T0146734

WOMEN
OF THE BIBLE
AND
CONTEMPORARY
WOMEN
OF FAITH

A Feminist Perspective

JACQUELINE GEORGE

WESTBOW
PRESS®
A DIVISION OF THOMAS NELSON
& ZONDERVAN

Scripture quotations marked NKJV are taken from the New King James Version.
Copyright 1982 by Thomas Nelson, Inc. Used by permission. All rights reserved.

WestBow Press books may be ordered through booksellers or by contacting:

WestBow Press
A Division of Thomas Nelson & Zondervan
1663 Liberty Drive
Bloomington, IN 47403
www.westbowpress.com
1 (866) 928-1240

Because of the dynamic nature of the Internet, any web addresses or
links contained in this book may have changed since publication and
may no longer be valid. The views expressed in this work are solely those
of the author and do not necessarily reflect the views of the publisher,
and the publisher hereby disclaims any responsibility for them.

Any people depicted in stock imagery provided by Thinkstock are models,
and such images are being used for illustrative purposes only.
Certain stock imagery © Thinkstock.

ISBN: 978-1-5127-9540-0 (sc)
ISBN: 978-1-5127-9539-4 (hc)
ISBN: 978-1-5127-9541-7 (e)

Library of Congress Control Number: 2017911214

Print information available on the last page.

WestBow Press rev. date: 9/21/2017

Dedicated to my Lord and Savior, Jesus Christ

All Scripture is given by inspiration of God,
and is profitable for doctrine, for reproof, for
correction, for instruction in righteousness.
—2 Timothy 3:16

CONTENTS

FOREWORD

T he pathways to ministry are many and varied. If there are any doubts about the ability of women to embrace the roles to which they have been called, all one has to do is take a quick look at the seats of power around the globe today. From Chancellor Angela Merkel in Germany to President Michelle Bachelet in Chile, from Prime Minister Theresa May in the United Kingdom to President Ellen Johnson Sirleaf in Liberia, all have triumphed around the subtle and not so subtle social, political, economic, and, yes, religious barriers they have faced from birth. But to name these women is not to minimize in any way the invaluable contributions that are being made every moment of every day by women all around the world. And this is not a fact that belongs only to the second decade of the twenty-first century! From time immemorial, women and girls have been unsung agents of change.

Dr. Jacqueline M. George's book compares some of these women who walked in biblical times to their contemporaries. While it richly describes their many selfless acts, it also captures the human struggles with which they were faced—be they Esther, Joan of Arc, or Malala. It highlights how often women have remained in the shadows, wielding quiet power that has been guided and strengthened only by their unyielding faith. And yes, it also discusses some who faltered and fell short of their promise. By far, however, Dr. George's book demonstrates the continuing thread of faith linking women across the generations, and how this has acted as a vehicle that drives major change.

An educator and a voice performance artist for more than thirty years, Dr. George has been passionate about her work in ministry, and writes with the deep conviction of her own faith. As a participant observer based on the parents we share, I humbly submit that she is also one of these women of faith. The purpose of Dr. George's book is to educate and to expand the discussion around women's roles as agents of change through ministry. The continuum that she establishes as she recounts women's engagement across biblical times to the present makes a significant contribution to the literature. It should be a must-read for students of biblical studies, women's studies, and those with a general interest in women's issues.

Monica A. Joseph, PhD
Advisor, Columbia School of Social Work
Tenured Associate Professor, City University of New York

ACKNOWLEDGMENTS

M ike, Denise, Tracy-Ann, Jason, Katrina, Shanni, Shaila, Kingston, Kelson, Keaton, Bernadette, Clarence, and all my brothers, sisters, nieces, nephews, and dear friends, I would not be who I am without your precious love. I thank God for all of you and for your constant support and encouragement.

I particularly want to thank Dr. Monica A. Joseph for her input in helping me crystallize and focus my thoughts as I embarked upon this work, and her continued support throughout. To all those who impacted my life and enabled me to grow spiritually and become rooted in Christ Jesus, I sincerely thank you.

Special acknowledgment must go to Let's Talk About Jesus Ministries and Pastors Oral and Phyllis Theobalds, my pastors, whose walk with the Lord has certainly helped me to strengthen and improve my own. Thank you for your unwavering faith and your constant prayers for me always. Saints of Let's Talk About Jesus Ministries, you are the best church family I know. Many thanks for your genuine love and all your prayers. Sister Dawn McFarquhar, thank you for your extra prayers and encouragement.

Pastor Bobbie Kpapharo, thank you and Bishop Peter Kpapharo for your love and friendship over the years. Mr. John Barrett, and Dr. and Mrs. Elvin Ames, your support and friendship are dearly cherished. Thank you. Dr. Yolanda Webster, thank you for demonstrating that it can be done. I certainly love and appreciate you. May God continue to shower His choicest blessings on each and every one of you.

Most of all, I thank the Most High God for life, health and strength, and for His guidance, grace, mercy, and faithfulness to me. His love is unfathomable.

INTRODUCTION

For centuries we have lived in a male-dominated society. Growing up, I continually heard the expressions "Ladies must be seen and not heard" and "It's a man's world." In 1966, well into the twentieth century, the rhythm and blues/soul singer, James Brown, wrote a song entitled "It's a Man's Man's Man's World." It was so much "a man's world" that he repeated "man's" three times. But do not be fooled. He went on to say the world was nothing if women were not a part of it.

Even today, many would like it to still be a man's world, but there is a time and season for everything. The "good old days" and the "boys' club" are still a virile force with which women must contend. A technology business owner and published writer notes, in a recent article, that during her early career, she had a series of handsome, charismatic bosses who were barely older than she was. But she hardly ever witnessed young women in similar positions of authority, no matter how qualified they were. She experienced firsthand being the most qualified candidate, yet being passed over for a male counterpart.[1]

Qumran, situated in the Judean desert in the West Bank, on the northwest shore of the Dead Sea, is the site of the discovery of the Dead Sea Scrolls in 1947. Scrolls of the books

---

[1] Hana Schank, "My Generation X Hillary Problem: I Know Why We Don't 'Like' Clinton," *Salon*, March 3, 2016, accessed March 4, 2016, http://www.salon.com/2016/03/03/my_gen_x_hillary_problem_i_know_why_we_dont_like_clinton/.

of Genesis, Exodus, Deuteronomy, Kings, and Isaiah, along with other canonical writings from the Hebrew Bible, were discovered. Noncanonical works, psalms, and hymns, and the Community Rule, a blueprint of regulations strictly followed by the sectaries, or members of the Essenes Sect, were also recovered.

The Essenes were a Jewish sect formed in 145 BC, during the period of the second temple. These precious scrolls were hidden in eleven caves by the Qumran Essenes, just before the Romans conquered Qumran in AD 68; the sect was routed and dispersed. In February 2017, a twelfth cave was discovered.

Flavius Josephus (AD 37–circa 100), a Jewish historian, documented the existence of the Essenes. They lived in poverty, humility, community, and purity, following a very rigorous, ritualistic, hierarchical, and communistic lifestyle. Flavius states that their piety toward God was exceptional. The desert Essenes did not marry. Though they did not fully condemn marriage, women were not allowed in the caves and tents they occupied.

Geza Vermes, speaking of the debate about celibacy among the Qumran sectaries, mentions "the idea of the presence of women among them appears incongruous ... the word *ishah*, woman, occurs nowhere in the Community Rule. Or rather, to be more exact, it is encountered once in the final Hymn, in the cliché, 'one born of woman.'"[2]

He also says, referring to the Cave 4 Damascus Document regulation that envisions married members, that the penalty for speaking against "the Fathers" was expulsion, but murmuring against "the Mothers" only warranted a ten-day atonement. "Silence concerning the presence of women seems therefore deliberate."[3]

In the beginning, the man, Adam, whom God had created and put in Eden, was alone. Long before James Brown, even from the very foundation of creation, God already knew man could

---

[2] Geza Vermes, introduction to *The Complete Dead Sea Scrolls in English* rev. ed. (London: Penguin, 2004), 34.

[3] Ibid.

not dwell alone. In fact, He said it was not a good thing, and He immediately found the solution. He created woman out of man.

> And the Lord God caused a deep sleep to fall on Adam, and he slept; and He took one of his ribs, and closed up the flesh in its place. Then the rib which the Lord God had taken from man He made into a woman, and He brought her to the man. (Gen. 2:21–22)

And so the first woman was created by God for a very special purpose: because He saw that Adam was lonely and that it was not good for Adam to be alone. God manifests His abounding goodness and mercy by immediately rectifying the problem of aloneness. One day Adam (Ish), was presented with this similar yet very different being, a gorgeous female whom he called Woman (Ishshah).

Adam must have been thrilled that God recognized that "it is not good that man should be alone; I will make him a helper comparable to him" (Gen. 2:18). What a wonderful solution! Only God could have found such a miraculous and perfect solution.

The Word of God states:

> Let your women keep silent in the churches, for they are not permitted to speak; but *they are* to be submissive, as the law also says. And if they want to learn something, let them ask their own husbands at home; for it is shameful for women to speak in church. (1 Cor. 14:34–35)

Paul was addressing a particular problem in the church at Corinth, where the women seem to have been disrupting the flow of the church service. "The talkativeness of women was allowed a place in the sacred assembly, or rather that the fullest liberty was given to it."[4] They were to be submissive, seeking answers to their questions from their husbands at home, not publicly.

In modern times, churches are filled with women. Women no longer want to keep silent. Women can no longer remain silent. Women no longer accept being second-class citizens, when time and time again their input has been vital in propelling change. Call it women's liberation, civil rights, or whatever name you may, women are standing up and being heard today, even in church. Women have had to step up to fill positions of authority. Some ministries are very ably run by women. It is a manifestation of what is taking place in the world.

Even as James Brown stressed it's a man's world, "nevertheless, neither *is* man independent of woman, nor woman independent of man, in the Lord" (1 Cor. 11:11). It took Eve to complete Adam, Sarah to complete Abraham, Rebekah to complete Isaac, and vice versa. Barak refused to go to battle unless Deborah accompanied him. Truly women have not just been heard throughout the ages. Women have been on the cutting edge of change, from Mother Eve in the Old Testament to Mother Teresa in contemporary times.

Men view feminism through completely different lenses. I once heard a gentleman try to describe what a woman meant to him. After much thought, he finally exclaimed, "A woman is a fluffy thing!" This person was trying to express how soft and gentle he felt a woman was and should be treated, but most women do not consider themselves fluff. In fact, many would be utterly offended by such a statement.

For the most part, women do not wish to be thought of as soft, fragile, and in need of protection, a view that still permeates and governs how men respond to women. Women do not accept the age-old tradition that a woman's place is in the home. Women are strong, resilient, and independent. They welcome opportunities to be a part of the discussion and decision-making process.

---

[4] John Calvin, *Commentaries on the Epistles of Paul the Apostle to the Corinthians vol. 1,* Chapter 14,trans. John Pringle (Grand Rapids, MI: Christian Classics Ethereal Library, n. d.), http://www.ccel.org/ccel/calvin/calcom39.xxi.v.html, 1 Cor. 14:34-40.

From the first woman to the woman of today, much has evolved, and so has feminism—not just gender equality, but equality for all. It is stated in the Declaration of Independence: "We hold these truths to be self-evident, that all men are created equal, that they are endowed by their Creator with certain unalienable Rights, that among these are Life, Liberty and the pursuit of Happiness." This is feminism succinctly defined. These are the unalienable rights that pioneers like Susan B. Anthony and Elizabeth Cady Stanton fought for—not just for women, but for all people, regardless of race, creed, or gender.

The women of the Bible were unique. Though they are far removed from present-day women, common threads unify women across eras—culture, motherhood, and issues and achievements that are unique to women. Edward Burnett Tylor (1832–1917), founder of cultural anthropology, defines culture as that complex whole, inclusive of belief, morals, law, knowledge, custom, art, and any habits or capabilities acquired by members of society. Merriam-Webster states it is the act of developing the intellectual and moral faculties, especially by education.

Herbert Lockyer, in his introduction to *All the Women of the Bible*, quotes H. V. Morton as saying we are likely to forget that since the age of Genesis, regardless of the inventions, the changes and the fashions of our time, people have not changed very much. This may be so, but many more women are aspiring to higher education and are a force to be reckoned with in the workplace, despite lower wages for the same job as their male counterparts. Fighting for the right to education for all children resulted in Malala Yousafzai being shot by the Taliban.

It has not always been easy for women to educate themselves. Margaret Ann Bulkley was born in Ireland near the end of the eighteenth century. Because she was a girl, it was inappropriate for her to go to medical school. In those days, that was a man's world.

With the aid of her uncle and a couple of his prominent friends, she crafted plans to attend Edinburgh Medical School in 1809, as "James Barry," male student. After graduation in 1812, "Barry" joined the army. For forty-six years, Margaret served as a doctor. She never married. Upon her death in 1865, her true identity was revealed. After 150 years, England has acknowledged that its first female doctor was Dr. James Barry, who pretended to be a man for forty-six years. This is an example of one of the challenges that women faced and, in various parts of the world, still face.

The woman, the bedrock of the family, was, is, and will continue to be, simply because God made it so. He knew His plan of action for procreation. Adam and Eve were commissioned to "be fruitful and multiply; fill the earth and subdue it; have dominion over the fish of the sea, over the birds of the air, and over every living thing that moves on the earth" (Gen. 1:28). All women may not choose to have children, and that is their right. This does not alter God's plan, nor does it exclude these women from making their voices heard as feminists.

There are 188 women named in the Bible, and many unnamed. Several can be ranked as women of faith—Jacob's wives, Leah and Rachel; Jochebed, the mother of Moses; Martha and Mary, the sisters of Lazarus; the Samaritan woman at the well; and the Syro-Phoenician woman, among others.

The biblical women I have chosen for this work are Eve, Sarah, Hagar, Rebekah, Tamar, Rahab, Ruth, Elizabeth, and the Virgin Mary from the bloodline of Jesus Christ; Hannah, Abigail, Deborah, Jael, Esther, and Jezebel. Nonbiblical women discussed include St. Joan of Arc, Mother Teresa, Oprah Winfrey, and Malala Yousafzai. These women were and are all strong decision makers with compelling stories to tell. Each made remarkable choices, and as their lives unfold, we see the consequences of their decisions, whether good or bad.

In each chapter, I have included a "Viewpoint" section, in which I look at whether faith was integral to the decisions each woman made; if and how lives were impacted, then and over time; and the lessons that can be gleaned by readers today.

Several issues unique to women are encountered in times of old and remain prevalent in the cultures of modern-day society—vices rooted in antiquity. Rape, incest, prostitution, barrenness, and poverty are as contemporary for us as they were for women in history. Many, sad to say, can identify with Tamar, Absalom's sister, when she pleaded with Amnon, her half brother, as he forced himself on her and then cast her out of his home. (2 Sam. 13:1–20).

There are those in the boys' club who still believe that they have total freedom to sexually abuse and denigrate women at will; women should just dance to the beat of the men's drum. Truly, the more things change, the more they remain the same.

The Great Commission was Jesus's last words to His disciples:

> Go therefore and make disciples of all the nations, baptizing them in the name of the Father and of the Son and of the Holy Spirit, teaching them to observe all things that I have commanded you; and lo, I am with you always, *even* to the end of the age. Amen. (Matt. 28:19–20)

Jesus was always doing His Father's business. He passed the baton to us. We now must win souls for the kingdom of God, if we profess to be His disciples. To this end, the appendices "The Confession of Faith," "Why Baptism" and "Where Would You Spend Eternity?" are extremely important elements of this book, showing how to reach out to those who have not yet, but may want to accept Jesus as Lord and Savior of their lives. This is the first and most crucial step of faith a Christian takes.

My book interprets the Bible from the perspective of a woman of faith, tracing the faith journeys of women in the Bible through contemporary times.

CHAPTER 1

EVE (CIRCA 4000 BC)

Adam's Rib

The first woman was specially created by God. God did not form Eve from the very dust of the earth, as He had formed Adam, but from one of Adam's ribs. Male and female He created them. Eve was beautiful. Lockyer claims that Eve was the most beautiful woman who ever lived. Her beauty far surpassed that of all the famous beautiful women throughout the ages, for God Himself created her. His divine perfection was reflected in her flawless beauty. When Adam beheld her, he exclaimed:

> "This is now bone of my bones
> And flesh of my flesh;
> She shall be called Woman,
> Because she was taken out of Man." (Gen. 2:23)

Adam and Eve were in fellowship with God, happy, carefree, rich, and powerful. God provided all they could ever need or want even before He created them and placed them in control in the garden of Eden. They were given this authority because God created them in His own image, superior to all other creatures that resided in Eden. The superiority of the created man is discussed by Boyce in his *Abstract of Systematic Theology* as follows:

> The highest organism is in man as an animal. He partakes with other animals of bodily firm [form], appetites, desires and passions. His bony structure is analogous to theirs, which approaches it closely, and yet with marked distinctions which manifest his yet higher life, with nobler capabilities. So, also, is it with his muscular covering or flesh, and his nervous system especially culminating in a brain of superior size and weight. Through the latter, man has capacity for superior intellectual powers over other animals.[1]

Adam and Eve were created superior to the other animals because of the dominion and special purpose God had planned for humanity. In conferring dominion,

> [God] commemorates that part of dignity with which he decreed to honor man, namely, that he should have authority over all living creatures. He appointed man, it is true, lord of the world; but he expressly subjects the animals to him, because they having an inclination or instinct of their own, seem to be less under authority from without.[2]

He also created them as free agents, giving them free will or the power of choice.

> And the LORD God commanded the man, saying, "Of every tree of the garden you may freely eat;

---

[1] James Petigru Boyce, *Abstract of Systematic Theology* (Louisville, KY: Chas T. Dearing, 1887), http://founders.org/library/boyce1/toc/, 158.

[2] John Calvin, *Commentaries on the First Book of Moses called Genesis: Commentary on Genesis* vol. 1, trans. John King (Grand Rapids, MI: Christian Classics Ethereal Library, n. d.), http://www.ccel.org/ccel/calvin/calcom01.pdf, 53-54.

but of the tree of the knowledge of good and evil
you shall not eat, for in the day that you eat of it
you shall surely die. (Gen. 2:16–17)

Eve was created to be her husband's helpmate. Adam had had
the opportunity to acquaint himself with all the animals and give
them names. All had mates of the same form, habits, and nature.
But none was suitable as his companion. Adam was superior to
all of them.

Eve is a Hebrew word meaning *life* or *living one*. God, therefore,
provided Adam with a live being comparable to his level, one with
whom he could relate, work and socialize. Adam could share his
life with Eve. God had created a suitable wife for him. In the words
of Stormie Omartian:

> He [God] could have created another man so
> Adam would have a golfing buddy, but He didn't.
> He created a woman who was "comparable to
> him." That means she wasn't merely an airhead
> with a great body. She *complemented* him. She
> *helped* him. And he needed her *companionship*
> and *support*. He needed someone to *communicate*
> with him on his level.[3]

The Woman You Gave Me

Eve, after being tempted and falling prey to sin, invited Adam
to help himself to the fruit he was forbidden to eat. Had he
stopped to think for a moment, he would have realized that Eve
was his wife, his Ishshah, not his God, his Creator, a role that far
superseded hers. In fact, there is no earthly comparison to God.
The words of Peter and the other apostles came centuries too late
for Adam: "We ought to obey God rather than men" (Acts 5:29).
Adam's rejection of God's infinite authority caused the greatest

---

[3] Stormie Omartian, *Praying Through the Deeper Issues of Marriage* (Eugene,
OR: Harvest House, 2007), 31.

domino effect, one that still continues today: all flesh, except Jesus Christ, is born slave to sin, "for all have sinned and fall short of the glory of God" (Rom. 3:23).

Elmer L. Towns speaks of Adam's transgression:

> Adam certainly was the man who had everything he needed or could ever want. Yet the tragedy of Adam's life is that he is remembered chiefly for the one day in his life when he lost it all. According to Scripture, Adam lived some 930 years (Gen. 5:5). Yet one day in his life was so significant that the world has never been the same since.[4]

Both Adam and Eve ate, but Scripture places the responsibility for that original sin squarely on Adam, because God's covenant was with him. He knew the price of disobedience was death, yet he erred with wide-open eyes. He knew he would surely die. He and his wife did not know that the seeds of disobedience and rebellion had already been planted by the devil, and they were caught in a web from which they could not extricate themselves, no matter how hard they tried.

Eve was by no means innocent. "Adam was not beguiled, but the woman being beguiled hath fallen into transgression" (1 Tim. 2:14). She allowed herself to be lured by the serpent. "Now the serpent was more cunning than any beast of the field which the LORD God had made. And he said to the woman, 'Has God indeed said, 'You shall not eat of every tree of the garden?'" (Gen. 3:1). Eve may have been the one who was accosted by the serpent and partook first of the fruit, but Adam harkened to her, although he had a covenant oath with his Creator. When we listen to and follow others who lead us astray, we reject the commandment of God. We should be cognizant that rejection of God's will leads to fulfillment of the devil's. God is the ultimate Judge of all.

---

[4] Elmer L. Towns, *A Journey Through the Old Testament: The Story of How God Developed His People in the Old Testament* (San Diego, CA: Harcourt Brace, 1989), 11.

The Wages of Sin

What caused Eve to be captivated by the devil and risk all the comforts and happiness of Eden? Pride, the first sin committed in heaven, and lust allowed the one who had dominion to be persuaded by the creature she dominated. She saw that the fruit from the tree was pleasant to the eyes and good for food, and that it could make her wise. She never thought about the fact that she was the superior being with a charge to keep: not to eat of the fruit of the Tree of Knowledge of Good and of Evil. She never thought about resisting the demonic attack through which she was influenced. The devil was at work in the serpent, there to devour, kill, and steal her joy and peace. Boyce observes, "The foundation for such desire might be found in the wish to gratify the lower appetites, or to attain higher exercise of the intellectual faculties."[5]

Fulfilling that desire and those appetites meant the immediate end of the rich, blissful life in Eden. James tells us to resist the devil and he will flee (4:7). We are told to be clothed in the full armor of God:

> Stand therefore, having girded your waist with truth, having put on the breastplate of righteousness, and having shod your feet with the preparation of the gospel of peace; above all, taking the shield of faith with which you will be able to quench all the fiery darts of the wicked one. And take the helmet of salvation, and the sword of the Spirit, which is the word of God. (Eph. 6:14–17)

Physically, a soldier must be fully prepared for war or become easy prey for the other side. In the same way, humanity must be spiritually prepared in life to battle any evil force. This is a necessity for survival for each and every Christian during our

---

[5] Boyce, *Abstract*, 185.

sojourn here on earth, "for the devil is going around like a roaring lion seeking whom he may devour" (1 Pet. 5:8). Our faith must be rooted in Jesus Christ; the battle is not carnal.

"Godliness with contentment is great gain" (1 Tim. 6:6). Paul says that he has learned to be satisfied, whatever state he is in. It is an exercise in futility trying to imagine what the world would be like if Eve and Adam had been content with all God provided for them in Eden, and had not obeyed the whim of the devil.

Adam and Eve went from innocent, carefree, and naked to guilty, fearful, and scrambling to cover their nakedness. Their knowledge instantly increased exponentially. If you are told that fire burns and you still put your hand in it, you will long remember the pain brought on by the experience. Hence obedience is learned by the things we suffer (Heb. 5:8). This holds true for us, but not for Adam and Eve. There was no way they could learn obedience after the fact and repair the broken covenant with their Creator. They were expelled from Eden.

In fact, they were helpless. But God in His infinite grace extended benevolence to them: He made them clothing, offered a sacrifice of atonement, and established a post-fall covenant with them. D. R. Dungan says: "They had failed to keep the first covenant, but this one they *would keep*, for they *could not help it*."[6] About the post-fall covenant, he says, "This contains a long struggle between the serpent and the seed of the woman, and the final victory in [on] behalf of humanity. In the meantime the race will have to be purified by toil, and saved by sorrow, from those iniquities which would drown them in their abominations."[7]

All flesh has been drawn into this vicious web of compulsion, a web from which no one can be extricated but for the love of God, nailing sin to the cross in the person of Jesus Christ, His only begotten Son. Paul says it better than most:

---

[6] D. R. Dungan, *Hermeneutics: A Text-Book*, 2nd ed. (Cincinnati, OH: Standard Publishing, 1888), 76.

[7] Ibid.

> For we know that the law is spiritual, but I am carnal, sold under sin. For what I am doing, I do not understand. For what I will to do, that I do not practice; but what I hate, that I do. If, then, I do what I will not to do, I agree with the law that *it is* good. But now, *it is* no longer I who do it, but sin that dwells in me. For I know that in me (that is, in my flesh) nothing good dwells; for to will is present with me, but *how* to perform what is good I do not find. For the good that I will *to do,* I do not do; but the evil I will not *to do,* that I practice. Now if I do what I will not *to do,* it is no longer I who do it, but sin that dwells in me. (Rom. 7:14–20)

And his utter frustration and disgust are manifested:

> I find then a law, that evil is present with me, the one who wills to do good. For I delight in the law of God according to the inward man. But I see another law in my members, warring against the law of my mind, and bringing me into captivity to the law of sin which is in my members. O wretched man that I am! Who will deliver me from this body of death? (Rom.7: 21–24)

This is the daily spiritual struggle humans must endure if they choose to live a holy, righteous and abundant life. This is the struggle, the legacy of Adam and Eve. Men and women must subdue the natural desire to sin. But God did not abandon us. He knows we are incapable to win this battle by ourselves, for we are constantly buffeted by the devil. We make supplication in the words of Jesus:

> "And do not lead us into temptation,
> But deliver us from the evil one." (Matt. 6:13)

He has made a way of escape, as Paul exclaims: "I thank God—through Jesus Christ our Lord!" (Rom. 7:25).

We join in this thanksgiving to our Lord and Savior Jesus Christ. It is unthinkable what our lives would be without His colossal sacrifice of Redemption.

Eve's Lost Legacy

Eve had a tremendous amount to lose when she willfully disobeyed the command of God. The legacy Eve lost that day in Eden included:

- The complete freedom and innocence she experienced in her initial relationship with Adam
- Sharing dominion with Adam over all of creation
- Her home
- Immortality
- A sinless nature
- The riches and bliss of Eden
- Personal fellowship and favor with the Creator

Dungan surmises: "Just what would have been the result of that covenant having been kept, we do not know, but all the glories of the primitive state would have certainly been secured."[8]

Eve's Legacy Inherited

Willful sin became a constant component of the fabric of human nature after the fall. Women inherited the curse proclaimed on Eve:

To the woman He said:

"I will greatly multiply your sorrow and your conception;

---

[8] Ibid.

In pain you shall bring forth children;
Your desire *shall be* for your husband,
And he shall rule over you." (Gen. 3:16)

No individual since Adam and Eve has come into the world except when birthed by a woman, including our Lord and Savior, Jesus Christ, born of a virgin. Every woman also had to contend with danger to her and her seed, from the serpent and his seed.

Eve, in her fallen state, finally learned how to look to her Creator, for God promised Eve and Adam that a Redeemer would come. God is infinitely just and faithful to His promises. He had to denounce humanity due to Adam's infidelity, but He would not do so without making a way that man can be redeemed. Many, many moons passed before the Seed mentioned in Genesis 3:15 was finally fulfilled.

Viewpoint

Eve, the matriarch of the human race, erred when she was enticed by the devil, and in turn encouraged her husband to taste of the forbidden fruit. She was the decision maker that day. She took matters into her own hands and yielded her power to the serpent. So did Adam, in accepting the fruit from her and eating of it. Since Adam was the one God first created to head the human race, God had given him specific instructions about the tree in the middle of the garden. Adam's lame excuse—that the woman whom God gave him made him eat of the fruit—did not atone for the gross error Adam made in forgetting the direct instructions of his Maker. As the leader, Adam had the opportunity to refuse to join Eve, or even to prevent her from making such a catastrophic decision.

> The baseness of human ingratitude is more clearly hence perceived, that when Adam and Eve knew that all animals were given, by the hand of God, into subjection to them, they yet suffered themselves to be led away by one of their own

slaves into rebellion against God. As often as they beheld any one of the animals which were in the world, they ought to have been reminded both of the supreme authority, and of the singular goodness of God.[9]

God's intended legacy for man was interrupted, and He had to find another way out. God, then, has given us a new covenant wrought through the infamous death on the cross of His only begotten Son, Jesus, the Christ. Man still has to keep his part of the covenant, obedience to God's Word. God laid out very meticulously in the Bible all His precepts and concepts by which we can live a righteous and holy life, and be in fellowship with Him if we so choose. In his meditations on the commandments of God, David wrote:

> You have commanded *us* to keep Your precepts diligently ... I will meditate on Your precepts, and contemplate Your ways ... Behold, I long for Your precepts; revive me in Your righteousness ... And I will walk at liberty, for I seek Your precepts ... I made haste, and did not delay to keep Your commandments ... I *am* a companion of all who fear You, and of those who keep Your precepts. The earth, O LORD, is full of Your mercy; teach me Your statutes ... Through Your precepts I get understanding; therefore I hate every false way ... I keep Your precepts and Your testimonies, for all my ways are before You. (Ps. 119: 4; 15; 40; 45; 60; 63–64; 104; 168)

This is David's commitment to diligently obey God's commandment to keep His precepts, His instructions. David

---

[9] John Calvin, *Commentary on Genesis* vol. 1, trans. John King (Grand Rapids, MI: Christian Classics Ethereal Library, n. d.), http://www.ccel.org/ccel/calvin/calcom01.pdf, 93.

accomplishes this by keeping company with those who fear God, meditating on His Word, and getting understanding of His ways. David's spiritual walk is a superb example to follow because not only David's, but all our ways are before God.

Stanford E. Murrell cites an unattributed quote: "If we have in the Word of God no infallible standard of truth, we are at sea without a compass, and no danger from rough weather without can equal to this loss within."[10]

Paul says, "For no other foundation can anyone lay than that which is laid, which is Jesus Christ" (1 Cor. 3:11). Because of Jesus's perfect submission to the will of His Father, "God also has highly exalted Him and given Him the name which is above every name, that at the name of Jesus every knee should bow, of those in heaven, and of those on earth, and of those under the earth, and *that* every tongue should confess that Jesus Christ *is* Lord, to the glory of God the Father" (Phil. 2:9–11). There is no other name under heaven by which man can be saved.

God's perfect plan was in place for mankind when He created the beautiful garden of Eden and placed our first parents there. "And they were both naked, the man and his wife, and were not ashamed" (Gen. 2:25). They were unblemished, in one accord, and obedient to their Creator, freely communicating with Him on a regular basis, taking no thought of their nakedness.

Suddenly, temptation and sin raised their ugly heads, forever quenching the peace and happiness of life in Eden. "The eyes of both of them were opened, and they knew that they *were* naked; and they sewed fig leaves together and made themselves coverings" (Gen. 3:7). For the first time, humanity knew what it meant to be mortified before each other and their Maker.

No longer could Eve and Adam go freely before God. Because of their disobedience, a veil was put between Almighty God and them, and therefore all mankind. Because of the obedience of the second Adam, Jesus, the veil to the Holy of Holies was rent, and we no longer

---

[10] Stanford E. Murrell, *A Foundation for Faith: An Introductory Study of Systematic Theology with References to the Baptist Confession of Faith of 1689* (1998), (Port Richey, FL: NTS Library, n. d.), http://www.ntslibrary.com/PDF%20Books/An%20Introductory%20Study%20of%20Systematic%20Theology.pdf, 73.

need a high priest to make atonement for us. But this was achieved at a great price, because there is no remission of sin without the shedding of blood. The Mosaic covenant clearly says this:

> Therefore not even the first *covenant* was dedicated without blood. For when Moses had spoken every precept to all the people according to the law, he took the blood of calves and goats, with water, scarlet wool, and hyssop, and sprinkled both the book itself and all the people, saying, "This *is* the blood of the covenant which God has commanded you." Then likewise he sprinkled with blood both the tabernacle and all the vessels of the ministry. And according to the law almost all things are purified with blood, and without shedding of blood there is no remission. (Heb. 9:18–22)

Jesus, at the last Passover meal He shared with His apostles, took bread, gave thanks to His Father, broke the bread, and gave it to the twelve, saying, "Take, eat; this is My body which is broken for you; do this in remembrance of Me" (1 Cor. 11:24). But He did not stop there. "In the same manner *He* also *took* the cup after supper, saying, 'This cup is the new covenant in My blood. This do, as often as you drink *it,* in remembrance of Me'" (1 Cor. 11:25).

The Law is a conditional covenant given by God to the nation of Israel, in the days of Moses. Deuteronomy 28 lists the blessings conferred if the Israelites were obedient to God, and the curses if they were not. Israel did not keep its part of this agreement, as documented in the book of Judges. Therefore a second covenant was necessary. This new covenant, once and for all, would save and restore man to fellowship with the Father, wrought through His only begotten Son, Jesus Christ.

Jesus's cleansing blood is the gift that keeps giving. Without It, we would still be stuck in our sins. He is the High Priest who made complete atonement for us by shedding His precious blood, from His agony in the garden of Gethsemane to Golgotha, Calvary, where He was crucified. With His arms stretched out and nailed to the cross, in the last throes of death, He said, "It is finished." What a victory for sinful man.

In spite of Adam and Eve and their sin of commission, God has made every provision for us to obtain the ultimate gift of life everlasting. It is His desire for mankind that none perish. It is the right of every individual, won for us through Christ. Matthew tells us: "Many are called, but few are chosen" (22:14). Paul tells us to make our election sure. Therefore, it behooves us to work with fear and trembling toward our salvation, so that our election is secure in Christ Jesus.

Eve in the New Testament

> For Adam was formed first, then Eve. And Adam was not deceived, but the woman being deceived, fell into transgression. Nevertheless she will be saved in childbearing if they continue in faith, love, and holiness, with self-control. (1 Tim. 2:13–15)

Paul is advising Timothy, a young minister whom he calls his true son in the faith. Timothy is facing tremendous challenges in restoring spiritual order to the church in Ephesus. Paul instructs him what to guard against, and how to organize in order to restore discipline.

Paul compartmentalizes the roles of men and women. Men are the leaders and teachers. Women should dress and behave in a distinctive way, not speak in church, and be submissive to the men. Women are not to exercise any authority over the men because it was Eve who was deceived by the serpent, not Adam. He was created first; she was created for him, and as the "weaker vessel," easily falls prey to temptation. Though Eve knew the facts, she totally disregarded God's supreme command. Yet God in His clemency extended to Eve, and therefore to all women, a way to be saved through the ordeal of childbearing, and by exercising humility and piety.

CHAPTER 2

THE ERA OF THE PRE-FLOOD WOMAN (CIRCA 2468 BC)

Wives, Sons and Daughters

Cain and Abel were born to Adam and Eve after their expulsion from Eden. Cain killed Abel, was cast out of the presence of God, moved to the land of Nod, and married.

> And Cain knew his wife, and she conceived and bore Enoch. And he built a city, and called the name of the city after the name of his son—Enoch. To Enoch was born Irad; and Irad begot Mehujael, and Mehujael begot Methushael, and Methushael begot Lamech. Then Lamech took for himself two wives: the name of one *was* Adah, and the name of the second *was* Zillah. (Gen. 4:17–19)

Zillah was the mother of Tubal-Cain and a daughter, Naamah. Seven generations after Eve, Adah and Zillah are the first names of women mentioned. We are told sons and daughters were born. Only the first son in each generation is named. Wives and daughters are not named. Adam and Eve had sons and daughters after Cain and Abel. Seth was the first son born after Abel.

In the Days of Noah

Lamech, when he was 182 years old, had a son he named Noah, stating, "This *one* will comfort us concerning our work and the toil of our hands, because of the ground which the LORD has cursed" (Gen. 5: 29).

Noah's world was very much like our contemporary world. Sin escalated over time after the fall from Eden. Early in the book of Genesis, we hear of a people whose evil intent was seen by God: "Then the LORD saw that the wickedness of man *was* great in the earth, and *that* every intent of the thoughts of his heart *was* only evil continually. And the LORD was sorry that he had made man on the earth, and He was grieved in His heart" (Gen. 6:5–6). What a declaration by the Creator about His creation!

Calvin comments on this passage, "Men were not only perverse by habit, and by the custom of evil living; but that wickedness was too deeply seated in their hearts, to leave any hope of repentance ... The world had then become so hardened in its wickedness ... that it was not the folly of a few days, but the inveterate depravity which the children, having received, as by hereditary right, transmitted from their parents to their descendants."[1]

When God could no longer accept the corrupt behavior of man, he chose Noah to do His will. It is humanity's sinful nature that caused God to tell Noah, "The end of all flesh is come before me; for the earth is filled with violence through them; and behold, I will destroy them with the earth" (Gen. 6:13). In fact, the way men and women lived proved that their hearts and minds were

---

[1] John Calvin, *Commentary on Genesis* vol. 1, trans. John King (Grand Rapids, MI: Christian Classics Ethereal Library, n. d.), http://www.ccel.org/ccel/calvin/calcom01.pdf, 174.

far removed from the things of God, and instead were burdened with the lust of the flesh and the things of the world.

The Bible tells us that the sons of God, beholding the dazzling beauty of women, indiscriminately chose themselves wives from among them, and children were born from these marriages. The sons of God were the descendants of Seth, the son of Adam and Eve. They were the pure worshippers of God, but they intermarried with the descendants of Cain and other profane races, thereby tainting the family line. The greater part of mankind, according to Calvin, prostituted itself by embracing depraved superstitions or harboring contempt for God, as opposed to worshipping the Creator, which was the purpose for which mankind was created.

Jamieson, Fausset, and Brown reiterate this sentiment—that the marriages of these parties, of contradictory practice and dogma, were positively infused with corruption. The women, they claim, had their own brand of religion that they exercised as wives and mothers, fatally influencing their households. Thus their offspring manifested the lowest immorality.[2]

> But Noah found grace in the eyes of the LORD. This is the genealogy of Noah. Noah was a just man, perfect in his generations. Noah walked with God. And Noah begot three sons: Shem, Ham, and Japheth. The earth also was corrupt before God, and the earth was filled with violence. So God looked upon the earth, and indeed it was corrupt; for all flesh had corrupted their way on the earth. (Gen. 6:9–12)

Post-fall men and women had that vein of corruption.

For 120 years, Noah preached his warning of devastation ahead, but no one listened to him. Polygamy flourished as they married and were given in marriage, ate and drank, and lived

---

[2] Robert Jamieson, A. R. Fausset, and David Brown, *Commentary Critical and Explanatory on the Whole Bible* (Grand Rapids, MI: Christian Classics Ethereal Library, n. d.), http://www.ccel.org/ccel/jamieson/jfb.x.i.vi.html, Gen. 6:2.

with lust and abandon, with no thought of tomorrow or of any repercussions. Such were the people of Sodom and Gomorrah.

Unfortunately, nothing much has changed into the twenty-first century. Satisfying the lusts of the flesh takes priority over obedience to the Word of God. So often we say, "Oh, God knows my heart." We can be unmistakably sure that He truly does.

A Remnant

God knew His pre-fall covenant with man had failed. He spoke to Noah about His coming judgment, adding, "But I will establish My covenant with you; and you shall go into the ark—you, your sons, your wife, and your sons' wives with you" (Gen. 6:18). Seven days before He initiated the deluge, He proffered this invitation: "Then the LORD said to Noah, 'Come into the ark, you and all your household, because I have seen that you are righteous before Me in this generation'" (Gen. 7:1). There were, therefore, at least four virtuous women left—Noah's wife and his sons' wives.

His sons were not practicing polygamists like their counterparts. Noah and his wife had done a good job of raising them. We are cautioned to train our children the way they should go, so when they grow, they will remember the training they received and not stray. Noah's three sons, Shem, Ham, and Japheth, did not follow the example of their peers of having multiple wives. They were brought up "in church," hearing the Word of God. Noah was busy preaching righteousness and doing God's will, and his righteousness extended to his entire household. "By faith Noah, being divinely warned of things not yet seen, moved with godly fear, prepared an ark for the saving of his household, by which he condemned the world and became heir of the righteousness which is according to faith" (Heb. 11:7).

Once the ark was loaded and the door shut, God began to send the floodwaters down until every man, woman, boy, girl, animal, and plant—everyone and everything—were buried under the waters as He had predicted. "I will destroy man whom I have created from the face of the earth, both man and beast, creeping thing and birds of the air, for I am sorry that I have made them" (Gen. 6:7). His Word had come to pass.

Viewpoint

Dungan tells us that polygamy was the curse of the earth in the days of Noah. Most of the sons of God were so overwhelmed by the beauty of women, they each chose several wives. This is the definition of polygamy. There are different forms of polygamy. Polygyny—one man having several wives simultaneously—is the most common. Polyandry—one woman having several husbands—is relatively rare. It is practiced, for example, in the Himalayas, where land is very scarce, and is employed as a means of preserving family inheritance.

Polygamy is legal, for example, in some countries in Africa and in China, and is partially practiced by some religious groups—Hindus, Jews, Buddhists, and Muslims—each group setting its rules and regulations. Among Christians, St. Augustine spoke out against polygamy, indicating that it was no longer necessary to continue this practice, once embraced by the ancients for the sake of procreation.

Here in the United States, polygamy is illegal, yet thirty to fifty thousand people are estimated to reside in polygamous relationships. Journalist Lisa Ling published a study exploring this culture called *Polygamy in America: Lisa Ling Reports*, which was featured on *The Oprah Winfrey Show*.

Ling explores the evolution of plural families in the United States, discussing with several individuals their experiences and expectations as members of polygamous relationships. Some wish for polygamy to be recognized and legalized, but God, in His infinite wisdom, first created one man and one woman, Adam and Eve, thereby sanctioning monogamy.

Ling's investigation brings to light information about the secret polygamous world of Warren Jeffs in Colorado City, Arizona. After his father's passing in 2002, Jeffs took over a breakaway Mormon sect, one of the largest polygamous groups in the United States, which calls itself the Fundamentalist Church of Jesus Christ of Latter-Day Saints (FLDS). His notoriety involving underage girls in sex, incest, and marriage earned him a place on the television program *America's Most Wanted.* In 2011, he was sentenced to life plus twenty years for two felony counts of child sexual assault.

The Jeffs case was a very high-profile court case in the United States of America in the twenty-first century, not in some distant, third world island. It is a stunning example of excessively autocratic, abusive behavior meted out to young girls and women. Wives and their daughters were not given the opportunity to make any decisions whatever, especially when it came to sexual relations. Plainly, they were at the mercy of the men. Young girls were forced to become sexually active at a very early age, and older women were tossed aside by their husbands.

There are several references to polygamous practices in the Old Testament, including Lamech, Moses, Abraham, Esau, Jacob, Hannah's husband Elkanah, David, and Solomon, among others. The twelve tribes of Israel, founded by the twelve sons of Jacob, were born to four different women. Solomon alone had three hundred wives and seven hundred concubines. In the book of Ecclesiastes, he came to the conclusion that all is vanity and vexation of spirit—"Let us hear the conclusion of the whole matter; Fear God and keep His commandments, for this is the whole duty of man" (Eccl. 12:13, KJV).

The September 11, 2001, attacks occurred in New York City at the World Trade Center. One individual who worked there, a beloved deacon who attended church with his family diligently, was among those who unfortunately perished. His wife and daughter, devastated with grief, were totally astonished to discover he had another family. The same situation surfaced when a former president of France, Francois Mitterrand, passed away.

These are isolated examples of a widespread practice, a practice that is still very much closeted in the Western world. Many who indulge in polygamy do not live in sects or communities. They reside in the general population. Polygamous behavior is one reason children grow up with one full-time parent, while the other is an occasional visitor. Often it is the father who is involved in multiple relationships in which the women do not live under the same roof.

It is refreshing to know that, although polygamy was declared the curse of the earth in the pre-Flood days, neither Noah nor his sons indulged in the practice. They feared the Lord. Paul clearly states, "A bishop then must be blameless, the husband of one wife, temperate, sober-minded, of good behavior, hospitable, able to teach" (1 Tim. 3:2). God rewarded Noah and his sons by allowing them and their wives to be the only humans saved from the Flood. Many were called by God through Noah, but the fewest of the few were chosen to enter the ark.

After the Flood, humanity again flourished, but Towns emphasizes that man's destiny was set on a course for irrevocable failure. There was another covenant, but due to man's inherently immoral nature, iniquity was evident even from his youth. Forever, insurgence would be a part of the corruption of man's fallen nature, initiated in the garden of Eden by Adam's disobedience in partaking of the forbidden fruit. Sin had become second nature to the human race. "And the Lord was sorry that He had made man on the earth, and He was grieved in His heart" (Gen. 6:6).

Mankind has not changed; day by day we still sin in thought, word, and deed, grieving our Maker. But God is faithful and impartial, and continually extends His great love and forgiveness to every single one of us. His mercy rains on the just and the unjust.

Centuries after Noah, Abraham was certain he did not want his son Isaac to marry a Canaanite woman. Abraham made his servant Eliezer swear to go to Abraham's relatives in Mesopotamia. Isaac, when his time came, did not want his son Jacob to marry locally either, and sent Jacob away to his mother's relatives in Padan Aram.

People of the post-Flood generations learned very little or nothing from the mistakes of their ancestors of the pre-Flood era. Today, well into the second decade of the twenty-first century, man's behavior is remarkably reminiscent of that of the men and women of Noahic times.

The Pre-Flood Woman in the New Testament

> But as the days of Noah *were*, so also will the coming of the Son of Man be. For as in the days before the flood, they were eating and drinking, marrying and giving in marriage, until the day that Noah entered the ark, and did not know until the flood came and took them all away, so also will the coming of the Son of Man be. (Matt. 24:37–39)

> By faith Noah, being divinely warned of things not yet seen, moved with godly fear, prepared an ark for the saving of his household, by which he condemned the world and became heir of the righteousness which is according to faith. (Heb. 11:7)

> By whom also He went and preached to the spirits in prison, who formerly were disobedient, when once the Divine longsuffering waited in the days of Noah, while *the* ark was being prepared, in which a few, that is, eight souls, were saved through water. (1 Pet. 3:20)

> And [God] did not spare the ancient world, but saved Noah, *one of* eight *people*, a preacher of righteousness, bringing in the flood on the world of the ungodly. (2 Pet. 2:5)

Moses follows the genealogy of Adam and his male descendants, but only Lamech's daughter, Naamah, is mentioned by name, pointing to the patriarchal society that existed. There is no account of any woman, none mentioned by name, but marriages were taking place, and daughters as well as sons were born. Four nameless women entered the ark: the wives of Noah and his sons Shem, Ham, and Japheth.

Ungodly men and women prevailed during this period. Hearts were turned to continual wickedness. Their preoccupation with life and their lack of faith in heeding the Word of God preached by Noah caused the entire pre-Flood generation to be caught spiritually off guard.

"So then faith *comes* by hearing, and hearing by the word of God" (Rm. 10:17). If we are not hearing and obeying God's Word, then we must be obeying the devil. He who has ears to hear should hear and heed the signs of the times, for perilous times are upon us.

CHAPTER 3

SARAI
(CIRCA 2156–2029 BC)

In Egypt

In Genesis 11:29–30, we hear about Sarai, the woman Abram marries. Sarai is a name that means *my princess*. When God commands Abram to get out of the country of his birth, he takes Sarai along. She was a beautiful woman to behold. At age sixty-five, she had never been pregnant. Her beauty was intact. Abram, therefore, felt compelled to ask that she present herself as his sister when they went to sojourn in Egypt due to the famine in Canaan. Abram told Sarai, "Indeed I know that you *are* a woman of beautiful countenance. Therefore it will happen, when the Egyptians see you, that they will say, 'This *is* his wife'; and they will kill me, but they will let you live. Please say you *are* my sister, that it may be well with me for your sake, and that I may live because of you" (Gen. 12:11–13).

Abram did not feel threatened as a brother, but feared greatly for his life as Sarai's husband. Pharaoh's men were always on the lookout for beautiful women to join their master's harem. Perhaps these men would have been unscrupulous enough to kill a husband to get his wife.

Marriage is sacred. The emotional connection between a husband and wife is totally different from that between a brother and sister. Hence Abram's carnal plan for his safety. According to Towns,

> Some have suggested that the wives of Egyptians were generally ugly and faded early. The women of Chaldea held their youth and beauty longer than other cultures. Others have noted that Egyptian women do not wear veils as is customary in other parts of the Near East. As the couple got closer to Egypt, the contrast between Sarai's physical beauty and the Egyptian women would have become increasingly obvious to Abram.[1]

Larry Wood also describes Sarah's beauty:

> When the Bible says someone is beautiful, it is reliable. Sarah was one of the most beautiful women in the world. Even at the age of 65 (derived from Genesis 12:4) Sarah was still beautiful, for this was only middle age for her, since she lived to be 127. Further, Sarah had not had her beauty marred by child bearing. Abraham knew that Sarah's beauty was a liability. So, in keeping with his role as leader, he devised a plan for Sarah's protection in the land of Egypt.[2]

Sarai was speaking the truth when she said she was her husband's sister, for they were of the same polygamous father, Terah. But she used this knowledge to misinform others about

---

[1] Elmer L. Towns, *A Journey Through the Old Testament: The Story of How God Developed His People in the Old Testament* (San Diego, CA: Harcourt Brace, 1989), 37.

[2] Larry Wood, "Sarah Attracts Worldly Attention", in *Sarah: Obedient Heroine of Faith*, 1997, revised Dec. 31, 2004 (Florida: biblenews1, 1995), accessed June 7, 2015, http://www.biblenews1.com/docs/sarah.htm.

her true identity, therefore supporting her husband but hiding the truth.

Abram's worst fears were corroborated. The Egyptians had an eye for beauty; when they beheld Sarai as she and Abram came into Egypt, the Egyptians saw that she *was* a very beautiful person. Pharaoh's princes also saw her, and without a doubt, recommended her to Pharaoh, who felt he had a claim to every beautiful woman. Abram's lovely wife was taken to his palace.

> The danger Sarai was in of having her chastity violated by the king of Egypt: and without doubt the peril of sin is the greatest peril we can be in. *Pharaoh's princes* (his pimps rather) *saw her, and,* observing what a comely woman she was, they *commended her before Pharaoh,* not for that which was really her praise—her virtue and modesty, her faith and piety (these were no excellencies in their eyes), but for her beauty, which they thought too good for the embraces of a subject. They recommended her to the king, and she was presently taken into Pharaoh's house ... in order to her being taken into his bed.[3]

While Sarai was forced to join Pharaoh's concubines, Abram was accumulating wealth in the land: "He [Pharaoh] treated Abram well for her sake. He had sheep, oxen, male donkeys, male and female servants, female donkeys, and camels" (Gen. 12:16).

God is merciful, and indeed our Father, for He extended His divine protection to these two history makers, in spite of the fabrication Abram concocted. God was on their side.

When He made His covenant with Abram, He said, "Do not be afraid, Abram. I *am* your shield, your exceedingly great reward"

---

[3] Matthew Henry, *Matthew Henry's Commentary on the Whole Bible* (Grand Rapids, MI: Christian Classics Ethereal Library, n. d.), http://www.ccel.org/ccel/henry/mhc1.Gen.xiii.html, Gen.12:14-20.

(Gen. 15:1). He plagued Pharaoh and his household with great plagues because of Sarai. Proverbs 6:29 states:

> So *is* he who goes in to his neighbor's wife;
> Whoever touches her shall not be innocent.

Pharaoh realized that Sarai was Abram's wife before it was too late. He returned her to her husband, reprimanded them, and had them escorted out of Egypt, with all the riches Abram had accumulated. Included in their acquired possessions was an Egyptian servant girl named Hagar, given to Sarai as her personal maid.

Leaning to Her Own Understanding

Ten years prior, God had promised that Abram would beget an heir from his own loins. Neither Abram nor his wife was still young, and Sarai had always been barren. There was no heir in sight, and no inkling in Sarai's mind that she would ever become pregnant.

But Sarai wanted a child. She devised a carnal plan to hasten the birth of a son—she gave her maid, Hagar to Abram. "So Sarai said to Abram, 'See now, the Lord has restrained me from bearing *children*. Please, go in to my maid; perhaps I shall obtain children by her.' And Abram heeded the voice of Sarai" (Gen. 16:2).

Towns comments that this occasion was the second of its kind recorded in Scripture. A great leader pursued his wife's carnal advice, resulting in a catastrophic outcome, forever to influence the human race. Of course, the first was Adam heeding the voice of his wife, Eve.

Adam and Abram had free agency; each made his own choice. The effects of the decision by both to obey their wives have left indelible marks on the human race. From Adam's decision came perpetual sin, in and for all mankind. From Abram's decision came perpetual havoc, especially in the Middle East. Even today, so many centuries later, the descendants of Ishmael by Hagar and

Isaac by Sarah are still warring. The angel of the Lord informed Hagar:

> "Behold, you are with child,
> And you shall bear a son.
> You shall call his name Ishmael,
> Because the LORD has heard your affliction.
> He shall be a wild man;
> His hand *shall be* against every man,
> And every man's hand against him.
> And he shall dwell in the presence of all his
> brethren." (Gen. 16:11–12)

Even from the womb, Ishmael was predicted to be a wild man, a man of strife, and a warmonger.

The Middle East is a bedlam of strife, hate, violence, and outright war in the twenty-first century. Every effort to achieve peace in this part of the world has failed. Civil war, torture, and unbelievable brutality continue to escalate daily.

On February 3, 2015, the world witnessed the brutal burning alive of Lieutenant Moaz al-Kasaesbeh, the Jordanian pilot captured by ISIS, the Islamic State in Iraq and Syria, also referred to as ISIL, the Islamic State of Iraq and the Levant. ISIS shamelessly flaunted the gruesome video on the Internet, even as they did the public beheadings of Americans: James Foley (August 19, 2014); Steven Sotloff (September 2, 2014); and Peter Kassig (November 16, 2014); as well as many more from several other nations.

A mass grave containing at least a hundred decapitated bodies was found in Iraq by soldiers on November 7, 2016, as they labored to recapture the town of Mosul from the clutches of ISIS. Many more Iraqis lost their lives, used as human shields by the enemy. This is just a small insight into the furor and retribution perpetuated by the terrorist group ISIS.

Man must tread carefully on this God-given earth, for the footprints he leaves behind matter. Some footprints are so gigantic and so deeply embedded that not even the floodgates of heaven can pour out enough water to wash them away. The

Flood did not remove sin from the earth, nor from the heart of man. The descendants of Abraham's sons, Ishmael and Isaac, have yet to learn to live at peace. Will it come in our lifetime? The greater question is, will it ever come?

Sarah (circa 2037 BC)

Sarai was barren, with no expectation of ever giving birth. At her age, she felt she was over the hill. She was not looking for any pie in the sky miracle. Hagar was young and fertile, Sarai's slave, who had no choice but to do Sarai's bidding. Thirteen years after Ishmael was born, certainly neither Abram nor Sarai were in the reproductive business, or so they thought.

But when Abram was ninety-nine years old, El Shaddai, Almighty God, revealed Himself to Abram (Gen. 17:1). God reassured him that he would have that promised heir, and modified his name from Abram to Abraham, which means *father of many nations*. As for Sarai, her name was changed from Sarai, *my princess*, to Sarah, *princess*. The change came with special blessings: "As for Sarai your wife, you shall not call her name Sarai, but Sarah *shall be* her name. And I will bless her and also give you a son by her; then I will bless her, and she shall be *a mother of* nations; kings of peoples shall be from her" (Gen. 17:15–16).

For the first time in His dealings with Abram, God included Abram's wife. She and her husband had to throw off "the old man" of corruption and put on "the new man" in the Spirit. This was the preparation of Abram's family line for the promised seed of Abraham, Isaac, and the promised Seed of Redemption, Jesus Christ. Abraham was instructed by God to walk blameless before Him.

Abraham and Sarah laughed when they received the news that they would have their very own child. Who would not? Sarah, then ninety years old, laughed to herself about having pleasure at this time of her life with her husband, who was quite old, a hundred years old to be exact. But this was not an impossibility with God.

At His promised time, Sarah and Abraham enjoyed their newfound happiness—and had Isaac, the son of their old age, named by God before his birth. God's Word does not return void but always accomplishes what He sets it to do. Sarah's shame at being barren was a thing of the past as she held her very own son.

At Isaac's weaning, a huge feast was held, and Sarah saw Ishmael ridiculing her son. With Isaac's birth, Ishmael lost his status as firstborn and the privileges attached to that title. Paul calls his laughter "persecution" (Gal. 4:29). Calvin states: "'He who was after the flesh persecuted the spiritual seed' (Galatians 4:29). Was it with sword or violence? Nay, but with the scorn of the virulent tongue, which does not injure the body, but pierces into the very soul.'"[4]

Sarah decided, through the will of God, to tell her husband to cast out the bondwoman and her son. She was adamant that Ishmael should not be heir with Isaac. God Himself had to intervene, for Abraham did not want to throw out his son Ishmael. God's will came through Sarah to her husband. Abraham was charged to heed the voice of his wife and send Hagar and Ishmael away. Isaac was the covenant child, the seed promised to Abraham so long before.

Testing and Obedience

Then God tested Abraham's faith. He demanded that Abraham take his only son, Isaac, and offer him as a burnt offering. There is no record of Abraham discussing this with his wife. No mention is made of Sarah having knowledge of or reacting to Abraham taking Isaac and leaving at daybreak, to worship and sacrifice unto the Lord. We are left to surmise what her response was. Edith Deen paints this picture: "At God's command, Abraham sets forth with their beloved Son of Promise to sacrifice him upon an altar. As Sarah sorrowfully watched her husband and son depart for

---

[4] John Calvin, *Commentary on Genesis* vol. 1, trans. John King (Grand Rapids, MI: Christian Classics Ethereal Library, n. d.), http://www.ccel.org/ccel/calvin/calcom01.pdf, 419

the mountains in the land of Moriah, we can imagine her anguish of heart."[5]

We know that when Isaac inquired about a lamb for the sacrifice, his father responded, "My son, God will provide for Himself the lamb for a burnt offering" (Gen. 22:8). If Abraham had truly sacrificed Isaac, Sarah might not have been able to withstand the pain of such a great loss. Perhaps Abraham never discussed it because he wanted to shield her. Maybe he kept silent because he felt she would discourage him from being obedient to what seemed a most unreasonable request from God—a request that he knew he had to fulfill, regardless of the consequences.

Abraham had come to that point of spiritual maturity that he knew he could trust his God implicitly. He learned to do so from the first time God told him to leave his country and go to a strange land. Some might think that because Sarah was his wife, Abraham was compelled to inform her. But this was not about a mundane matter. As high priest of his home, he was in charge of all spiritual decisions. If God had wanted Sarah to know, He would have specified this to Abraham. From a spiritual standpoint, there was no breach of marital fidelity, no disingenuousness on the part of Abraham in his dealings with Sarah.

Sarai's Weaknesses

- She depended on the carnal instead of the spiritual.
- She misrepresented the truth to help Abram in Egypt.
- Impatient, she defiled her marriage bed by initiating a polygamous relationship with Hagar and Abraham, hoping a son and heir would be born.
- She treated Hagar harshly when Hagar began to disrespect her after Hagar had become pregnant.
- She misused her power.

---

[5] Edith Deen, *All of the Women of the Bible* (San Francisco: HarperCollins, 1955), 15.

Sarah's Strengths

- She was loyal to her husband in spite of the lie he asked her to tell.
- God changed her name to Sarah, the mother of many nations, thereby including her in the covenant for the first time.
- She gave birth at age ninety, fulfilling God's name for her as the mother of many nations.

Viewpoint

Sarah, the only woman in the Bible whose age was revealed, was beautiful and loyal to her husband, to the point of distorting the truth to protect him when they sojourned in Egypt. Unfortunately, that carnal plan for protection went awry, and Sarai ended up as a member of Pharaoh's harem because of her awesome beauty. In the end she was released to her husband, with a reproof from Pharaoh, because God had afflicted Pharaoh's household.

God is always there to help us pick up the pieces when we mess up. He alone knows the thoughts that He thinks toward us—thoughts of peace and not of evil, to give us a future and a hope (Jer. 29:11). He intervened on Abram and Sarai's behalf. He made a way for her to get back to her rightful place beside her husband. He had great plans for her life. Sarai was sixty-five years old at that time.

For all her life, she had been unable to have children. God promised her husband that they would have their own child. Ten years later, when there was still not a child in sight, she fabricated her own carnal plan for an heir. Sarai could not wait for God to have His way in her life, though His promise to Abraham was clear.

This is a grave shortcoming of human beings. We fail to realize that God has *His plan* to execute in *His time*. Most of our lives we seem unable to wait upon the Lord, a reflection of the weakness of our faith. Sometimes, when God's response or solution is not equivalent to what we hope it will be, we tend to express dissatisfaction. We should remember Sarah and Abraham. "Is anything too hard for the Lord?" (Gen. 18:14).

His Word promises,

> But those who wait on the LORD
> Shall renew *their* strength;
> They shall mount up with wings like eagles,
> They shall run and not be weary,
> They shall walk and not faint. (Isa. 40:31)

Sarah had to learn to wait on God. So does this present generation, enthusiasts of instant gratification.

God is faithful, and all His promises are "yea and Amen." Indeed, Eccl. 3 mentions there is a time and a season for everything under heaven: "a time to laugh" (v.4) and "a time to be born" (v.2). What God promised Abram, He finally brought to pass when Sarah, at the ripe old age of ninety, birthed her only child, their son and heir, Isaac. God's Word had finally come to pass.

Sarah's joy brimmed over. God can make the barren conceive, no matter the age. He did it for Sarah, Rebekah, Rachel, Hannah, Manoah's wife, the mother of Samson, and Elizabeth, mother of John the Baptist. How many countless others have been blessed this way? Only God has the answer.

The oldest woman on record for becoming pregnant in contemporary times is seventy-year-old Omkari Panwar of India, who was delivered of twins in 2008, by emergency cesarean. Her husband was seventy-seven years old. The record states that she became pregnant by in-vitro fertilization (IVF) and an egg donor.

Sarah was twenty years Omkari's senior, and Abraham was one hundred years old, yet God's Word was all it took to fulfill the promise He had made to them. Nothing is too hard for God. He can make the barren womb bring forth fruit. He rewards the faith of those who diligently seek Him, for He is God Almighty, immutable and awesome in every way.

Contemporary women experience some of the same issues that Sarah and Hagar encountered, and have even more to deal with today. There are many who have difficulty becoming pregnant; some are pursued for their beauty like Sarai; some have to put up with the polygamous behavior of their spouses; and many are exploited because of lust. In numerous places, the issue of sex slaves is of epidemic proportion, and young children and adults are being traded for money to sate the appetites of sexual perverts. There are others who have dedicated time and resources to advocate for this population, especially the children who are grossly and brutally violated. While in a variety of ways life has improved for women, there is still too much left to be desired.

If we truly come to know our Maker and fear Him, such abuse will not be, for we will strive for holiness, righteousness, and justice; we will demonstrate not just love of self but of others. Such atrocities will not have a chance to flourish because we will remember Jesus's teaching, to treat others the way we want to be treated.

But, as the Bible says, the heart of man is wicked, and things will wax worse and worse in this world. However, accountability to God will be required of each of us. One day, we shall all stand before Christ at the judgment seat. God is immutable.

Sarah's Death and Burial

Sarah was living in Kirjath Arba, the city of Arba, later renamed Hebron, when she died at the age of 127. Though she was living in the city, Towns says that Sarah died still in fellowship with God. These great men and women had steadfastly followed God by faith, and were still controlled by that faith. He summarizes Sarah's life thus:

> For 62 years she followed her husband in his pilgrimage of faith. For 37 of those years she had been the mother of the promised seed. Because of her fidelity to her husband in the unusual course of his life, she had several unique opportunities to see God at work and became the matriarch of

the people of God, Israel, and an ancestress to
the Messiah.[6]

Abraham and Isaac mourned her death. When it was time
to bury Sarah, Abraham was offered the best burial sites, and
purchased the cave of Machpelah and a field owned by Ephron
ben Zohar, a Hittite. This cave became known as the Cave of the
Patriarchs. Sarah was the first to be buried there.

Sarah in the New Testament

"And not being weak in faith, he did not consider his own
body, already dead (since he was about a hundred years old),
and the deadness of Sarah's womb" (Rom. 4:19). Paul references
Abraham's steadfast faith in God as an example to the Romans.
Abraham did not look at the circumstances—that he and Sarah
were quite old. God had said his heir would come from his own
loins. Abraham's faith was credited to him for righteousness
because he trusted God's Word: "For this *is* the word of promise:
'At this time I will come and Sarah shall have a son'" (Rom. 9:9).

Abraham and Sarah already had Ishmael by Hagar, but Paul
tells the Romans that Ishmael was not the seed just because he
came from Abraham. Ishmael was of the children of the flesh,
not of the children of God. Isaac was of the children of promise
and counted as the seed: "nor *are they* all children because they
are the seed of Abraham; but, 'In Isaac your seed shall be called'"
(Rom. 9:7).

"By faith Sarah herself also received strength to conceive
seed, and she bore a child when she was past the age, because
she judged Him faithful who had promised" (Heb. 11:11). Paul
states that faith is the evidence of things not seen, the substance
of things hoped for. The elders obtained a good testimony
because of their faith. Sarah is one of these elders whose faith in

[6] Elmer L. Towns, *A Journey Through the Old Testament: The Story of How God Developed His People in the Old Testament* (San Diego, CA: Harcourt Brace, 1989), 80.

God should inspire us. Though she originally laughed at the idea that she could become pregnant at age ninety, Sarah's faith grew tremendously when she came to understand that God's Word is unquestionable and will come to pass.

"Sarah obeyed Abraham, calling him lord, whose daughters you are if you do good and are not afraid with any terror" (1 Pet. 3:6). In cautioning wives to obey their husbands, Peter mentions Sarah. She called Abraham lord and subjected herself to him. As the daughters of Abraham, the father of many nations, wives should pattern their lives after the holy women of old, who trusted in God. Their clothing was the incorruptible beauty of a quiet and gentle spirit, which was precious in God's sight, and they had nothing to fear. God was indeed making preparation for the coming of His Son, Jesus Christ.

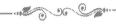

CHAPTER 4

HAGAR,
THE SURROGATE
(CIRCA 2081 BC)

Sarai's Plan

During the famine in Canaan, Abram and Sarai went to Egypt temporarily. When they returned home, Hagar, a young slave, was in their company, given to Sarai as her personal maid.

One day, life changed drastically for this young girl—her mistress, Sarai, gave Hagar as wife to Abram, Sarai's husband. Hagar was not excited about this turn of events. She was a young girl, far from home, perhaps with dreams of having a family of her own. Now she was not only the slave wife of her mistress's husband, but the surrogate mother of their child. She was angry and despised her mistress. Towns in his discussion states that Hagar saw Sarai as responsible for her abuse. Sarai retaliated and was even harsher.

Hagar's Flight

The name Hagar means *flight*. When the pregnant slave could not deal with the harshness any longer, then, true to her name, she fled from her mistress, which was not the correct thing to do. She, after all, was Sarai's slave, and her duty was to be obedient to her mistress. But during that desperate period of escape, she was ministered to by God Himself. "The Angel of the Lord" appeared to Hagar. He was not just an angel, says Towns, but God Himself appearing to Hagar in one of His many pre-incarnate, or Christophany forms—Jesus Christ, present in the Old Testament. This particular appearance was not made to a prophet of God, but to a troubled Gentile woman.

A Christophany is an Old Testament appearance of a special angel. Jesus Christ, the Second Person of the Trinity, appears as the representative of the Father on earth, as the Angel of God, foreshadowing the New Testament coming of the Son of God in the form of sinful man. His role as Savior is clearly seen in Hagar's story. He saved Hagar from committing a grave act of disobedience, and restored her to her rightful place, even as He has restored us to fellowship with the Father.

The Lord spoke to Hagar: "Hagar, Sarai's maid, where have you come from, and where are you going?" (Gen. 16:8). She replied, "I am fleeing from the presence of my mistress Sarai" (Gen. 16:8). El Roi, meaning *God sees*, revealed Himself to Hagar and truly saw everything. His love and forgiveness shone through as He admonished her to return to her mistress and be submissive. She was instructed that her unborn child was to be called Ishmael, meaning *God hears*.

The God who sees and hears reached out to this pregnant slave girl and gently encouraged her to return to her rightful place in Abram's camp. The Bible speaks of the obedience of servants to their masters and vice versa. We must learn, whatever state we are in, to be content and to do all things as unto the Lord.

> Bondservants, be obedient to those who are
> your masters according to the flesh, with fear

and trembling, in sincerity of heart, as to Christ; not with eyeservice, as men-pleasers, but as bondservants of Christ, doing the will of God from the heart, with goodwill doing service, as to the Lord, and not to men, knowing that whatever good anyone does, he will receive the same from the Lord, whether *he is* a slave or free. (Eph. 6:5–8)

There is also a warning for mistresses like Sarah: "And you, masters, do the same things to them, giving up threatening, knowing that your own Master also is in heaven, and there is no partiality with Him" (Eph. 6:9).

Hagar's child was born and given the name Ishmael, as God commanded. Ishmael grew up as the heir, the promised seed of Abram. Abram was eighty-six years old when Ishmael was born and enjoyed the pleasure of fatherhood. But God's promise was yet to be fulfilled. When Abram, now Abraham, was ninety-nine, God again visited him and brought that promise of a covenant child to pass.

Isaac was born and was recognized as the seed of promise. Hagar and Ishmael were cast out from Abraham's camp when Sarah found Ishmael making fun of Isaac. Sarah immediately demanded that her husband get rid of them, regardless of the fact that Sarah was the one who had initiated the polygamous relationship with Hagar.

Outcasts

Hagar and Ishmael, who was now around seventeen years old, were given bread and water and sent on their way by Abraham. When the water ran out, Hagar cried hopelessly. She left Ishmael about fifty feet away in a shady area and sat across from him, because she did not want to see her son die. They both cried aloud, partly because of thirst, and partly because of the cruel turn of events in their lives—the agony of being thrown out so unexpectedly, with no provision made for their welfare, no one to turn to, and no place to go. Anyone who has been evicted from his or her home, especially when children are involved, can fully empathize with Hagar and Ishmael.

The God who hears and sees again came to their rescue. He heard the voice of the lad crying out. "Suffer the children to come unto Me," says Jesus. "Then the angel of God called to Hagar out of heaven, and said to her, 'What ails you, Hagar? Fear not, for God has heard the voice of the lad where he *is*. Arise, lift up the lad and hold him with your hand, for I will make him a great nation'" (Gen. 21:17–18).

Hagar was in a state of despair. Her strength and faith were waning; she thought Ishmael would die. She apparently forgot that during her first encounter with the Lord, she was told her descendants would greatly multiply. Ishmael, therefore, was destined to live.

Ishmael's pain was likewise great. It seemed he had gone from riches to rags instantly. After enjoying firstborn status for thirteen years, he was demoted, then thrown out from his home. How cruel could fate be? He and his mother were dying of thirst. He cried the louder. The name Ishmael means *God hears*. God heard his pleas. God showed Hagar a well that she had overlooked, and she and her son were revived.

This was the second time God demonstrated His faithfulness to Hagar. When she was pregnant, she was encouraged to return to Sarai and humble herself. Nearly twenty years later, when she and her son were cast out of the only home they knew, God made sure they departed without being deprived of the blessings He had in store for them. Ishmael was not the covenant son, but he was Abraham's son; he became a great nation, as God had promised his father.

Viewpoint

Hagar left her homeland to be Sarah's personal maid, and ended up becoming the slave wife of Abraham. Today, there are young girls who are lured from their homes, locally and abroad, and end up enslaved, mistreated, and abused for several years, if not a lifetime. Many are overjoyed when they believe they are getting a lucrative position in a foreign country or another state, to start a better life. Then they discover that the job description they were given was totally erroneous—simply bait for naive, unsuspecting individuals. Some women are forced into prostitution against their will.

Like these young women, Hagar never dreamed that life in Canaan would turn out the way it did, and that she would have to lie with her mistress's elderly husband and become pregnant by him.

Hagar was an Egyptian slave and idol worshipper. God, indeed, is no respecter of persons, and will have mercy on whomever He chooses. He spoke to Hagar on two separate occasions, both times when she was at her lowest, deeply distraught, and in critical need of physical assistance and divine guidance. Dr. Alexander Whyte (1836–1921) describes her situation in these terms:

> Hagar, by reason of the extremity of her sorrow; by reason of the utter desolateness and brokenness of her heart; and by reason of the sovereign grace and abounding mercy of God— Hagar, I say, stands out before us in the very foremost rank of faith, and trust, and experience, and assurance. Hagar, to me, stands out among God's very electest saints. Hagar has only one or two who can stand beside her in her discovery of God, in her nearness to God, in her face-to-face fellowship with God, in the instructiveness, in the comfort, and in the hopefulness of her so close communion with God ... The best and the most blessed of them all was not more or better blessed than was Hagar the polluted outcast on

her weeping way to Shur. The pure in heart shall see God.[1]

Whyte has done a magnificent job of summarizing Hagar and her walk, as she comes to know and experience firsthand the God of mercy, our Father, and His supreme benevolence. He gave her the strength to turn back to a life she abhorred. And when time came for her to finally depart from Abraham's camp, God gave her the strength to take her son and leave.

God instructed Hagar to return to the camp when she first ran away because she was with child and needed care. Besides being God compassionate, He is God of order. The time had not yet come for Hagar to leave. Sometimes God does not remove the problem, but allows us to go through. Hagar had to go through.

Although Sarah initiated a carnal plan through Hagar, Hagar's child was considered Abraham's and Sarah's. Hagar was the surrogate mother. She did not have the authority to make any decision about Ishmael's life. This was left to the recognized parents. When Ishmael misbehaved toward his younger half brother, Abraham knew it was time to break ties with Hagar and her son. Isaac had to be established as the covenant seed. The children of darkness must be separate from the children of light. This time the Angel of God did not instruct them to return to camp. He took care of their needs.

Each of us must learn to cry out to God for ourselves. We are told by Jesus to ask, and it will be given to us; seek, and we will find; knock, and it will be opened to us. "For everyone who asks receives, and he who seeks finds, and to him who knocks it will be opened" (Matt. 7:8). We must make our requests to God. He desires that we should.

Though still a youth, Ishmael was old enough to cry out to God for himself. God always meets us at our need. He heard Ishmael's pleading and let Hagar know He had not left her or

---

[1] Alexander Whyte, *Bible Characters Vol.1–6: The Complete Edition* (Dallas, TX: Primedia E-launch, 2011), https://books.google.com/books?id=N9MqM7g DomAC&printsec=frontcover&source=gbs_ge_summary_r&cad=0#v=onep age&q&f=false, chapter 13.

her son forsaken. He promised her, just as He had promised Abraham, that Ishmael would become a great nation and have an inheritance. He then opened her eyes to reveal the well of water, when they were literally dying of thirst. What an on-time God we serve, the Provider of all our needs!

Hagar believed God's Word unconditionally. Ishmael became a great nation; to him were born twelve princes.

Hagar in the New Testament

> Tell me, you who desire to be under the law, do you not hear the law? For it is written that Abraham had two sons: the one by a bondwoman, the other by a freewoman. But he *who was* of the bondwoman was born according to the flesh, and he of the freewoman through promise, which things are symbolic. For these are the two covenants: the one from Mount Sinai which gives birth to bondage, which is Hagar— for this Hagar is Mount Sinai in Arabia, and corresponds to Jerusalem which now is, and is in bondage with her children—but the Jerusalem above is free, which is the mother of us all. (Gal. 4:21–26)

This reference is made by Paul in addressing the Galatians. He chides them:

> O foolish Galatians! Who has bewitched you that you should not obey the truth, before whose eyes Jesus Christ was clearly portrayed among you as crucified? This only I want to learn from you: Did you receive the Spirit by the works of the law, or by the hearing of faith? Are you so foolish? Having begun in the Spirit, are you now being made perfect by the flesh? Have you suffered so

many things in vain—if indeed *it was* in vain? (Gal. 3:1–4)

Paul is realizing that all his labor in teaching the Galatians, whom he calls his little children, seems to have been in vain. All men are justified, saved through Jesus Christ, by His death on the cross. The Galatians were drifting from Paul's teachings of grace through Jesus Christ, back to the Jewish Law, the five books of Moses. Spiritually, Paul feared for them and the church in Galatia.

In the passage from chapter 4, Paul uses metaphorical language to amplify his point, contrasting Ishmael and Isaac, Abraham's two sons. Hagar and Sarah represent the two covenants, under Moses and under Christ. The Mosaic covenant was the Law given to Moses on Mount Sinai, which Paul calls Hagar. The Law typifies bondage or sin, "knowing that a man is not justified by the works of the law but by faith in Jesus Christ, even we have believed in Christ Jesus, that we might be justified by faith in Christ and not by the works of the law; for by the works of the law no flesh shall be justified" (Gal. 2:16).

Ishmael, the son of Hagar, a slave woman, is representative of the Law, which enslaves a man if he adheres to it. Paul compares the earthly Jerusalem to Hagar, Mount Sinai, referencing the spiritual condition of bondage of the Jews, who claimed to be the children of Abraham, yet continued to hold fast to the old covenant, the Law of Moses.

Isaac, the promised son, born of the free woman Sarah, represents the Jerusalem above, the new covenant in Jesus Christ. Sarah is called the mother of us all, because both Jew and Gentile are unconditionally welcome to join in the abundant life of spiritual freedom, walking in the righteousness of Jesus Christ. It is even as the Pledge of Allegiance states, "one nation under God, indivisible, with liberty and justice for all."

As Gentiles, we were not a people, but were grafted into the body of Christ, due to the unbelief or rejection of Christ by the Jews. But the day is coming when the Jews will be restored in Christ: "And they also, if they do not continue in unbelief, will be grafted in, for God is able to graft them in again" (Rom. 11:23). All should "pray for the peace of Jerusalem: 'May they prosper who love you'" (Ps. 122:6).

O foolish Galatians, and all those who have not yet fully understood, do not be overcome or bewitched by false doctrines and laws. True freedom comes only in Jesus Christ. Paul tells the Corinthians that there is liberty where the Spirit of the Lord is, and the Lord is the Spirit. What a privilege to be free!

CHAPTER 5

REBEKAH
(CIRCA 2026 BC)

Eliezer's Successful Mission

Abraham's last recorded words were a conversation between him and his trusted servant in Genesis 24. He did not want his only son Isaac to marry anyone from Canaan; neither did he want Isaac to go to the land that he himself had left. So resolute was Abraham that he made his servant swear to go to the city of Nahor, in Mesopotamia, and find a worthy bride among his own relatives for his beloved son. The servant, Eliezer, took several gifts of his master's wealth, and beseeched God's kindness that his journey would be successful and he would be led to the perfect bride for Isaac.

He went to a well where women of the city came to draw water. Eliezer had a very special prayer—that the young lady who offered water to him and his camels would be the chosen bride for Isaac. We constantly say, "God is always on time." As soon as Eliezer finished his prayer, Isaac's future bride appeared—Rebekah came, pitcher on shoulder, to the well. God demonstrated to Eliezer that He hears and answers prayers.

Eliezer discovered Rebekah was fully qualified to be Isaac's bride: she was the granddaughter of Milcah and Nahor, Abraham's brother; and the daughter of Bethuel, son of Milcah and Nahor. Rebekah was good-looking, friendly, gracious, hardworking, hospitable, respectful, and modest. These are all the qualities to be a great wife.

When her father and her brother Laban heard what Abraham's servant had to say, they responded, "The thing comes from the LORD; we cannot speak to you either bad or good. Here *is* Rebekah before you; take *her* and go, and let her be your master's son's wife, as the LORD has spoken" (Gen. 24:50–51). If we learned to accept God's will as easily as Bethuel and Laban did, many of us would experience much less pain and sorrow, and would have greater success in our lives.

Though young, Rebekah, whose name means *loops of a rope*, was mature enough to make her own decision to follow the servant and meet her husband-to-be. She did not waver, but firmly made up her mind to go with Eliezer, whom she had so graciously served at the well.

He accepted no delay, although the family asked that Rebekah stay for another ten days: "Do not hinder me, since the LORD has prospered my way; send me away that I may go to my master" (Gen. 24:56). Rebekah was consulted, and her decision, "I will go," was accepted. She and Eliezer set off on their nine-hundred-mile journey.

When her husband was pointed out to her, Rebekah demonstrated modesty by alighting from her camel and covering her face, so it would not be seen before her marriage. Eliezer told Isaac all that had taken place on his journey. Then Isaac took Rebekah to his mother Sarah's tent and consummated their marriage. She became his wife, and he loved her. Abraham must have breathed a sigh of relief that his dearly loved son was now safely married.

History Repeats Itself

There was a famine in the land like in the days of Abraham and Sarah. Isaac and Rebekah went to Gerar to Abimelech, the

Philistine king. History repeated itself in an uncanny way with Isaac, whose experience was almost identical to that of his father Abraham in Egypt.

God communed with Isaac and told him to remain in Gerar, and not go to Egypt, as Abraham and Sarah had. He renewed with Isaac the covenant He had made with Abraham: "I will be with you and bless you, for to you and your descendants I give all this land" (Gen. 26:3). Isaac heeded God and remained in the land of Gerar with his wife Rebekah.

Like father, like son: "And the men of the place asked about his wife. And he said, 'She *is* my Sister'; for he was afraid to say, '*She is* my wife,' *because he thought,* 'lest the men of the place kill me for Rebekah, because she *is* beautiful to behold'" (Gen. 26:7).

Like Sarah, Rebekah was very beautiful, and Isaac feared for his life if he was known to be her husband. Both Abraham and Isaac fabricated a lie and asked for their wives' support. Scripture does not say explicitly that Isaac asked Rebekah to say she was his sister, but he himself told the men, and she went along with the lie.

After Isaac and Rebekah had been in Gerar for a long time, one day King Abimelech, looking through a window, discovered Isaac being affectionate to Rebekah. "And Abimelech said, 'What *is* this you have done to us? One of the people might soon have lain with your wife, and you would have brought guilt on us.' So Abimelech charged all *his* people, saying, 'He who touches this man or his wife shall surely be put to death'" (Gen. 26:10–11). Fortunately for Rebekah, she did not go through the same experience as Sarah, who was taken into Pharaoh's harem as one of his concubines.

Answered Prayer

Again, Rebekah, like Sarah, was barren. The Bible says Isaac "pleaded with the Lord for his wife." Rebekah did not have to wait until she was old. God heard the cry of her husband. She found herself pregnant with twins, twenty years after her marriage. As the twins struggled within her, she inquired of the Lord, "If all is well, why am I like this?"

And the Lord said to her:

> "Two nations *are* in your womb,
> Two peoples shall be separated from your body;
> *One* people shall be stronger than the other,
> And the older shall serve the younger." (Gen. 25:23)

Rebekah never shared with Isaac what God revealed to her about the twins in her womb. What was ahead for her unborn sons was a lifetime of favoritism shown by both parents, a prolonged struggle between the boys, and a continued, continuous battle between their descendants, the Israelites and the Edomites, still manifesting today, so many centuries later.

Rebekah brought forth twin boys. The firstborn was red and hairy and was named Esau. His twin brother came out holding on to Esau's heel and was called Jacob. Isaac loved Esau, but Rebekah loved Jacob. Esau was a hunter, a man of the field, but Jacob was a "wholesome man," abiding in tents.

Esau, at forty, was ready for marriage, as his father had been at that age. He took two wives: Judith, the daughter of Beeri the Hittite; and Basemath, daughter of Elon the Hittite. "And they were a grief of mind to Isaac and Rebekah" (Gen. 26:35). Rebekah and Isaac were grieved over Esau's choice of polygamous marriage, something they had never entertained. Isaac had no other wife but Rebekah, despite the fact that polygamy was rampant all around. He was satisfied with the wife of his youth. In contemporary times, more young men would do well to adopt Isaac's lifestyle.

Stolen Blessings

As Isaac grew old, and his eyes dimmed with age, he called Esau. Isaac asked Esau to go to the field, hunt venison, and prepare some of the savory food that he loved. Isaac wanted to eat and then bless his firstborn.

Rebekah heard and sprang into action. She told Jacob what she had overheard—Isaac was about to bless Esau before he died.

> Now therefore, my son, obey my voice according to what I command you. Go now to the flock and bring me from there two choice kids of the goats, and I will make savory food from them for your father, such as he loves. Then you shall take *it* to your father, that he may eat *it,* and that he may bless you before his death. (Gen. 27:8–10)

Jacob complained to his mother that his brother was a very hairy man, and he was the complete opposite. His father could feel the difference. Jacob would seem like a deceiver and bring a curse upon himself. Rebekah retorted, "Let your curse *be* on me, my son; only obey my voice, and go, get *them* for me" (Gen. 27:13). "Then Rebekah took the choice clothes of her elder son Esau, which *were* with her in the house, and put them on Jacob her younger son. And she put the skins of the kids of the goats on his hands and on the smooth part of his neck" (Gen. 27:15–16).

Rebekah gave Jacob the savory food she had cooked to take to Isaac, and Jacob played right along. When his father asked who he was, he responded, "I am Esau your firstborn; I have done just as you told me; please arise, sit and eat of my game, that your soul may bless me" (Gen. 27:19).

Isaac was surprised that Esau had found venison so quickly. Because of his failing eyesight, he asked his son to come near, so he could feel him to know whether he was Esau or not.

Rebekah had thought of everything to make sure her husband was convinced he was blessing his firstborn. Jacob was dressed to deceive, wearing his older brother's clothes and with goat skins on his hands and neck. Isaac remarked that the hands were the hands of Esau, but the voice was that of Jacob. Isaac again asked if he was really his son Esau. Jacob kept up the charade: "I am." And when Isaac had eaten, indeed he blessed Jacob with the blessing of the firstborn—and rightly so, because Esau had sold his birthright to Jacob. Isaac was not privy to the prophecy given to Rebekah about the younger being served by the older.

Esau, justifiably, was angry at his brother Jacob, and vowed to kill him as soon as mourning was over for their father. Rebekah got wind of the fate that awaited her beloved Jacob, and again conceived a plan to secure his safety. She told him to flee to her brother in Haran and remain there until Esau's wrath subsided. But she told a different story to her husband: "I am weary of my life because of the daughters of Heth; if Jacob takes a wife of the daughters of Heth, like these *who are* the daughters of the land, what good will my life be to me?" (Gen. 27:46).

The daughters of Heth were descended from the great-grandson of Noah. Ham, Noah's son, had four sons: Cush, Mizraim, Put, and Canaan. The sons of Canaan were Sidon and Heth. Heth became the father of the Hittites. Canaan, the youngest son of Ham, was cursed by Noah, his grandfather. After the Flood,

> Noah began *to be* a farmer, and he planted a vineyard. Then he drank of the wine and was drunk, and became uncovered in his tent. And Ham, the father of Canaan, saw the nakedness of his father, and told his two brothers outside. (Gen. 9:20–22)

> So Noah awoke from his wine, and knew what his younger son had done to him. Then he said:

> "Cursed *be* Canaan;
> A servant of servants
> He shall be to his brethren." (Gen. 9:24–25)

The Bible does not specify how many generations were cursed, but Esau's wives were Hittites and did not please Isaac or Rebekah. Consequently, Rebekah used this ploy to separate Jacob and Esau. Isaac later called Jacob and sent him away to his mother's relatives in Haran.

Viewpoint

Parents must be aware of the emotional well-being of their children, who are extremely sensitive and can easily discern partisan behavior. Esau, when he learned that Jacob had received the blessing that supposedly was for him, was pathetically wounded. He begged his father to bless him also: "'Have you only one blessing, my father? Bless me—me also, O my father!' And Esau lifted up his voice and wept" (Gen. 27:38).

From the very beginning, Isaac loved Esau, but Rebecca loved Jacob. Even in her womb, when the twins were wrestling, she went to the Lord for answers. Rebekah was the first woman we hear of who sought God and asked Him for some explanation of her condition. This illustrated initiative, self-confidence, and faith in God.

Rebekah, as a mother, must have loved both her sons, but to be forewarned is to be forearmed. She was told that Jacob would be the leader. Probably because of that prior knowledge, she preferred Jacob over Esau, and did all she could to help him become successful in life. Determination can be added to the list of attributes for Rebekah.

> She prized the blessing as invaluable; she knew that God intended it for the younger son [Gen. 25:23]; and in her anxiety to secure its being conferred on the right object—on one who cared for religion—she acted in the sincerity of faith; but in crooked policy—with unenlightened zeal; on the false principle that the end would sanctify the means.[1]

Nevertheless, Rebekah used deceit, and aided and abetted her son Jacob to do the same. She accomplished what she set

---

[1] Robert Jamieson, A. R. Fausset, and David Brown, *Commentary Critical and Explanatory on the Whole Bible: The Old Testament* (Grand Rapids, MI: Christian Classics Ethereal Library, n. d.), http://www.ccel.org/ccel/jamieson/jfb.x.i.xxvii.html, Genesis, chapter 27, Gen. 27:6-10.

out to do, but paid a very heavy price. She not only betrayed her husband and cheated her firstborn out of his father's blessing, but had to live with this guilt, Isaac's disgust, and Esau's hurt and animosity for the rest of her life. She, by her unjustifiable, treacherous, and wholly inexplicable intervention for her favorite son, says Lockyer, stained her solemn marriage. Most of all, she had to send her beloved Jacob away from her, since his life was at stake. This must have been her greatest pain, for she never laid eyes on her favorite son again. Whatever the choice, there is always a price.

Whether we agree or disagree with the way life unfolded for Esau and Jacob, or with Rebekah's fraudulent means to an end, God's design was fulfilled. He was already setting up the plan of man's redemption, and He knew the bloodline into which His Son would be born. Esau was the firstborn, but the weaker of the two. He disinherited himself when he forfeited his birthright for a bowl of lentil stew. Paul says of Esau, "Lest there *be* any fornicator or profane person like Esau, who for one morsel of food sold his birthright" (Heb. 12:16).

Esau was fully cognizant of his action when he sold his birthright to his twin brother. On the other hand, this was in God's supreme plan. Jacob, whose name means *supplanter* or *deceiver*, went on to become Israel, and fathered the twelve tribes of Israel. Jesus Christ is called the Lion of the Tribe of Judah. Judah was Leah's fourth child.

Many years later, Jacob returned with his family, still afraid that Esau was angry. He approached Esau, bowing to the ground seven times until he reached him, "But Esau ran to meet him, and embraced him, and fell on his neck and kissed him, and they wept" (Gen. 33:4). Rebekah would have been ecstatic.

Rebekah in the New Testament

And not only *this*, but when Rebecca also had conceived by one man, *even* by our father Isaac (for *the children* not yet being born, nor having done any good or evil, that the purpose of God according to election might stand, not of works but of Him who calls), it was said to her, "The older shall serve the younger." As it is written, "Jacob I have loved, but Esau I have hated." (Rom. 9:10–13)

Rebekah's actions, though deceptive, were in keeping with the divine plan of God. He promised David that David would always have one of his descendants on the throne. This was fulfilled in Jesus Christ, our Lord and Savior. Rebekah in her time played the part that God had destined for her in His plan of salvation, ever since Adam and Eve broke that first covenant in the garden of Eden. She was buried in the Cave of the Patriarchs with her husband Isaac.

CHAPTER 6

TAMAR (CIRCA 1900 BC)

Motherhood Denied

Judah, one of the sons of Israel (Jacob), visited an Adullamite named Hirah. While there, he saw Shua, a Canaanite woman, married her, and had three sons by her: Er, Onan, and Shelah. Judah took Tamar, whose name means *palm*, as wife for Er, his firstborn. But Er was destroyed by God because he was evil, and Tamar was left a widow.

According to the Law, Onan was next in line to marry Tamar and raise up children to his dead brother. His father sent him to do exactly that, "but Onan knew that the heir would not be his; and it came to pass, when he went in to his brother's wife, that he emitted on the ground, lest he should give an heir to his brother. And the thing which he did displeased the LORD; therefore He killed him also" (Gen 38:9–10).

Tamar was bereaved of a second husband and still childless. Childbearing is a right that most women look forward to when married, and this was especially true for biblical women. Her father-in-law told her to remain a widow in her father's house until his youngest son, Shelah, was old enough to become her husband. She was obedient and did so. But when Shelah was grown, Judah reneged on his word, and Tamar remained a widow. According to Wesley, this custom of marrying the brother's widow was later made one of the laws of Moses in Deuteronomy 25:5.

Tamar Plays the Harlot

Tamar had run out of patience and was determined not to remain childless. She formulated a strategy and brought it to fruition. She took off her widow's garments, donned the apparel of a harlot, wrapped herself in a veil, and sat in an open place where Judah could see her. It was sheep-shearing season, and she was told her father-in-law was on his way to Timnah with a friend, Hirah, for the shearing. Shua, Judah's wife, had already passed away.

Judah mistook the woman he saw by the roadside for a harlot, and requested her services. Tamar had hidden her face; he had no inkling that he was speaking to his daughter-in-law.

She asked him what would he give her to have that honor. Judah promised a young goat from his flock. Tamar asked for the pledge of his staff, signet, and cord until the goat was delivered, and Judah agreed. Tamar lay with him and conceived by him. Then she went back to wearing her garments of widowhood. When Judah sent the promised goat by Hirah, in exchange for the pledge he had left, there was no harlot to be found. Judah decided not to pursue the issue.

There are always gossipers around, and in time Tamar's pregnancy began to show. Scripture does not name who said it, but three months later, Judah was told, "Tamar your daughter-in-law has played the harlot; furthermore she *is* with child by harlotry" (Gen. 38:24). Judah was outraged: "Bring her out and let her be burned!" he exclaimed.

The Bible uses the figure of irony marvelously in this account. Tamar remained silent until she was brought out. She knew she held the trump card, so to speak, and Judah was in for the shock of his life. She sent the items of the pledge to him with a very specific message: "'By the man to whom these belong, I *am* with child.' And she said, 'Please determine whose these *are*—the signet and cord, and staff'" (Gen. 38:25).

Judah recognized his belongings and had to admit that Tamar was more righteous than he was. He knew she had deceived him because he failed to keep his promise to give her his youngest son, Shelah, to wed. The Word of God says he never knew her again.

Viewpoint

Luckily for Tamar, she only pretended to be a harlot, so that she could claim what was rightfully her lot—motherhood. But there is a saying that what is done in the dark will be brought to light. Or is it that your sins will overtake you? Both these situations confronted Judah. Tamar's brilliant request for pledge items left no room for doubt about how she managed to be a virtuous widow and be with child at the same time. She was obedient and faithful to her father-in-law's instructions, but he broke the covenant he made.

> Despite Tamar's unorthodox methods, she was a woman of integrity who risked her life to fulfill her duty to herself and her family. She knew she had the right to a child, and she knew that her first husband Er had the right to an heir. Once again, God's plan unfolded through the unorthodox actions of a woman.[1]

As always, we cannot ask God what His plan and purpose are, or how He will bring them to pass. Neither do we know who He will use. Tamar, a Canaanite woman, is another example of the mixed genealogy of the Messiah (cf. Rahab and Ruth), says Utley. God knows the very end before the beginning.

---

[1] Elizabeth Fletcher, *Women in the Bible: Tamar & Judah, Bible Story*, 2006, accessed June 30, 2015, http://www.womeninthebible.net/women-bible-old-new-testaments/tamar-judah/.

Tamar found that she was bearing twins. The same that occurred with Rebekah, at the birth of Esau and Jacob, happened to Tamar.

> When she was giving birth, that *the one* put out *his* hand; and the midwife took a scarlet *thread* and bound it on his hand, saying, "This one came out first." Then it happened, as he drew back his hand, that his brother came out unexpectedly; and she said, "How did you break through? *This* breach *be* upon you!" Therefore his name was called Perez. (Gen. 38:28–29)

Tamar in the New Testament

> The book of the genealogy of Jesus Christ, the Son of David, the Son of Abraham: Abraham begot Isaac, Isaac begot Jacob, and Jacob begot Judah and his brothers. Judah begot Perez and Zerah by Tamar, Perez begot Hezron, and Hezron begot Ram. Ram begot Amminadab, Amminadab begot Nahshon, and Nahshon begot Salmon. Salmon begot Boaz by Rahab, Boaz begot Obed by Ruth, Obed begot Jesse, and Jesse begot David the king. (Matt. 1:1–6)

Tamar makes it into the genealogy of Jesus Christ through the birth of her son Perez by Judah, one of the twelve sons of Israel. Twin sons were born to her after she played the roles of both harlot and adulteress. Matthew Henry comments that including an adulteress is a mark of humiliation. Not only is such an event in the genealogy of Jesus Christ, but no effort is made to hide it; no veil is drawn over it. He left His heavenly kingdom, humbled Himself, and was born of woman. Jesus took on the form of sinful flesh, and is able to draw even the greatest of sinners to Him.

CHAPTER 7

RAHAB, THE HARLOT (CIRCA 1405 BC)

Used of God

The Bible tells us, "Then the woman took the two men and hid them" (Josh. 2:4). And this was not all the woman did. She made up a lie about the whereabouts of these two men, strangers she had never met.

That is what harlots do for a living. They meet strangers all the time. This woman, Rahab of Jericho, was a harlot. But God can use even the harlot to bring His will to pass. God used Rahab to help deliver Jericho into the hands of His people. The name Rahab means *wide*, *large*, or *broad*.

Rahab was going about her own business when two spies whom Joshua had sent to scout out the land came to her. The king of Jericho commanded his men to inquire about the strangers. Rahab blatantly lied and protected the people of God. She hid them with the flax stalks on her roof. Before they fell asleep, she came to them and said:

> I know that the LORD has given you the land, that
> the terror of you has fallen on us, and that all the

inhabitants of the land are fainthearted because of you. For we have heard how the LORD dried up the water of the Red Sea for you when you came out of Egypt, and what you did to the two kings of the Amorites who *were* on the other side of the Jordan, Sihon and Og, whom you utterly destroyed. And as soon as we heard *these things,* our hearts melted; neither did there remain any more courage in anyone because of you, for the LORD your God, He *is* God in heaven above and on earth beneath. (Josh. 2:9–11)

Covenant

Only God could reveal Himself to a harlot in such a way that she could say, "For the Lord your God, He is God." All authority in heaven and on earth is in His hands to accomplish His will. Because of this acknowledgment, Rahab was moved by faith, hid the men, and led them to safety. She knew the hand of God was against the people of Jericho and had only one request: "Now therefore, I beg you, swear to me by the LORD, since I have shown you kindness, that you also will show kindness to my father's house, and give me a true token, and spare my father, my mother, my brothers, my sisters, and all that they have, and deliver our lives from death" (Josh. 2:12–13).

Kindness begets kindness. The men, obviously very grateful for her help, promised her; they gave their word that when they finally took possession of the land, "we will deal kindly and truly with you."

Rahab's house was situated near the city wall, and she assisted the two spies by letting them through a window by a rope. She cautioned them to flee to the mountain to avoid their pursuers. She advised them further to remain there three days, until it was safe to go on their way. Rahab made sure their safety was not compromised.

To honor her request, the men also gave Rahab explicit instructions:

> We *will be* blameless of this oath of yours which you have made us swear, unless, *when* we come into the land, you bind this line of scarlet cord in the window through which you let us down, and unless you bring your father, your mother, your brothers, and all your father's household to your own home. So it shall be *that* whoever goes outside the doors of your house into the street, his blood *shall be* on his own head, and we *will be* guiltless. And whoever is with you in the house, his blood *shall be* on our head if a hand is laid on him. (Josh. 2:17–19)

This covenant the spies made with Rahab the harlot was unambiguous to the last detail. She had shown them compassion and protected them when they were vulnerable in a land they did not know, and they agreed to return the favor.

Every covenant has a clause to render it void if one of the parties does not fulfill his part. The men stipulated what this would be: "If you tell this business of ours, then we will be free from your oath which you made us swear" (Josh. 2:20). Rahab's reply, "According to your words, so be it" (Josh. 2:21).

Joshua and the children of Israel had the victory, as the Lord had proclaimed, and Joshua commanded the two spies to remove Rahab and her household: "Go into the harlot's house, and from there bring out the woman and all that she has, as you swore to her" (Josh. 6:22). A man's word is his bond. Rahab had kept her part of the covenant. They executed theirs.

Rahab's house was easy to discern because she was obedient and tied the scarlet cord in her window. Obedience brings blessings, and Rahab, by an act of faith, saved not just herself but her entire household. This is the Lord's promise—if we are faithful, He will save us and our households.

God is in the blessing business. Rahab, though she lived a life of harlotry, experienced the compassion of a forgiving Father.

He does not care how we come to Him, only that we trust Him enough to come. He has given to each of us a measure of faith, even as big as a mustard seed. Rahab put her little faith to good use to obtain salvation for her entire household. Faith can move mountains. In Rahab's case, faith could save an entire household of unbelievers.

Viewpoint

Most of us would look down on a harlot, but we thank God for His mercies that endure forever. In His words,

"For My thoughts are not your thoughts,
Nor are your ways My ways." (Isa. 55:8)

"Though your sins are like scarlet,
They shall be as white as snow;
Though they are red like crimson,
They shall be as wool." (Isa. 1:18)

Rahab was in the profession that, at the turn of the nineteenth century, became known as the world's oldest profession. Prostitution is still alive and well in society today. In fact, it is estimated that prostitution has escalated into a $186 billion per year industry, with China being the greatest consumer at a whopping $73 billion in revenue and a population of five million prostitutes. The United States comes in fifth, with $14.6 billion and one million prostitutes.[1]

There is a movement on to decriminalize prostitution in several countries. As one writer puts it, "[T]he barriers some try to draw between various forms of prostitution in order to make it acceptable are imaginary. Prostituted children become adults, trafficked women work in 'legal' massage parlours and in the windows of the red light district of cities like Amsterdam, and

---

[1] Havocscope, LLC, "Prostitution Statistics," *Havocscope: Global Black Market Information*, accessed March 31, 2016, http://www.havocscope.com/prostitution.

illegal prostitution is rife in places that have legalized or fully decriminalized the industry."[2]

Recently, the British asked that prostitution be legalized, because men need more sex than women, intimating that it is fine for men to obtain sex wherever, whenever, and however they can. God made humanity higher than the other animals. He expects that our behavior will not be repulsive, wayward, and vile, but that we will conduct ourselves as worthy of being called His children. Lust is numbered among the seven deadly sins.

"Let no one say when he is tempted, 'I am tempted by God'; for God cannot be tempted by evil, nor does He Himself tempt anyone. But each one is tempted when he is drawn away by his own desires and enticed. Then, when desire has conceived, it gives birth to sin; and sin, when it is full-grown, brings forth death" (James 1:13–15). God has given freedom of choice to every person. When lust rules our lives, it means we choose sin and choose to live in spiritual darkness.

There was a young man who gave testimony of being addicted to pornography for many years. One day, he was introduced to Jesus and accepted Him as Lord and Savior of his life. In other words, he became a Christian. This young man then found the strength to turn off the television and reject his former desires. Instead, he turned on the radio and listened to the Word of God. The young man's life took a complete 180-degree turn. He was later ordained as an evangelist, and continued to labor to tell others about Jesus Christ, the Man who made such a remarkable difference in his life. Today, he is a walking Bible, literally able to quote Scripture accurately from memory, including the book and chapter of every verse. He is completely immersed in the Word of God. It is awesome what God can and will do when we wholeheartedly submit ourselves to Him.

Though it was her livelihood, Rahab did not solicit the men who came to her from Joshua. She recognized that they

---

[2] Meghan Murphy, "Prostitution by Any Other Name Is Still Exploitation," December 12, 2013, *Vice*, accessed March 31, 2016, http://www.vice.com/read/decriminalizing-prostitution.

were different and favored by God. All she requested was that they return her act of kindness and be merciful to her and her household.

Rahab was used by God for His purpose because He looked beyond all her faults and saw her needs, and that she was sincere in heart. She was the ideal one to choose. It left little room for suspicion, because men always came to her for their needs. This time, God had need of her to protect His chosen people. Of ourselves, we can do nothing. Rahab acted as protector because God chose to use her to fulfill the promise He had made to Abraham: that Abraham's seed would inherit the land.

Rahab's kindness to strangers was an act of faith. Her obedience to the instructions given sealed the victory for her. If we learn to walk in faith and obedience to His will, we too will experience the hand of God moving in our lives. It is therefore imperative that we cultivate a personal relationship with Jesus Christ from an early age, so our faith can be nourished and strengthened. Faith comes when we hear the Word of God.

King Saul learned the hard way that "obedience is better than sacrifice." He foolishly lost the kingdom after Samuel had specifically made known to him God's instructions: "Now go and attack Amalek, and utterly destroy all that they have, and do not spare them. But kill both man and woman, infant and nursing child, ox and sheep, camel and donkey" (1 Sam. 15:3).

But Saul listened to the people. They kept the best oxen and sheep and other things, to sacrifice to God. He also kept Agag, king of the Amalekites, alive. As Samuel told Saul, his lack of obedience caused God to tear the kingdom from him. God expects His instructions to be executed as He wishes. Saul and his men leaned to their own understanding, and Saul irrevocably suffered the consequences.

Rahab did not allow anyone to interfere with what she had to do. As Mother Teresa, a twentieth-century saint, said, "Do not wait for leaders. Do it alone, person to person." Rahab did it alone, under the guidance of the Most High God.

Rahab in the New Testament

Rahab is mentioned in the genealogy of Jesus Christ:

> The book of the genealogy of Jesus Christ, the Son of David, the Son of Abraham: Abraham begot Isaac, Isaac begot Jacob, and Jacob begot Judah and his brothers. Judah begot Perez and Zerah by Tamar, Perez begot Hezron, and Hezron begot Ram. Ram begot Amminadab, Amminadab begot Nahshon, and Nahshon begot Salmon. Salmon begot Boaz by Rahab, Boaz begot Obed by Ruth, Obed begot Jesse, and Jesse begot David the king. (Matt 1:1–6)

Salmon was one of the princes of the house of Judah, the fourth son of Israel. Lockyer, in *All the Women of the Bible*, claims that Salmon was one of the two spies sent out by Joshua to spy out the land of Jericho.[3] His gratitude for the safe haven provided by Rahab turned into love, and he married her. This indicates that she ended her life of harlotry, forgiven of her sins and cleansed by God. Boaz, the great-grandfather of David, was born to them.

Rahab is included in the book of Hebrews, numbered among those who demonstrated great faith—patriarchs like Abraham, Isaac, Jacob, Moses, and others. Who would believe that a harlot could gain such high honor? But when God blesses, no man can curse, and whom He exalts, no man can debase.

> By faith the harlot Rahab did not perish with those who did not believe, when she had received the spies with peace. (Heb. 11:31)

---

[3] Herbert Lockyer, *All the Women of the Bible* (Grand Rapids, MI: Zondervan, 1988).

> Likewise, was not Rahab the harlot also justified
> by works when she received the messengers and
> sent *them* out another way? (James 2:25)

Faith without works is dead. For faith to come alive, there must be works. Rahab was able, by the grace of God, to bring her faith to good works. She protected the two spies, saved her household, and earned a place in the genealogy of Jesus Christ. Who can fathom the mind of God!

CHAPTER 8

DEBORAH
(CIRCA 1150 BC)

Judge and Prophetess

Deborah is the only female judge featured in the book of Judges. In Hebrew, Deborah means *bee* or *spirited woman*, and so she was. She was a wife, a famous counselor, a speaker of wisdom, and a prophetess who judged Israel for many years. She finally became a great deliverer of her people. Deen states that she demonstrated womanly excellence and was deemed a mother who surfaced to great leadership in Israel because her faith in God was complete and unwavering. She also had the ability to motivate others to develop this kind of faith.

The children of Israel were again out of the will of God when Judge Ehud died. They had returned to being disobedient to His commandments and doing whatever they wanted, including serving other gods. But when they felt the oppression of the enemy, they always cried out to God. This time, it was twenty years of tyranny by Jabin of Hazor, king of Canaan, and Sisera of Harosheth, the commander of Jabin's army. The enemy had nine hundred iron chariots and a great army—formidable to say the least—and God's chosen people were sorely afraid.

The Israelites looked to Judge Deborah to rescue them, yet another time, from the oppressive enemy. She called on Barak, the leader of the army of Israel, and gave him God's command— deploy troops against the enemy and He will deliver Sisera into his hands. But Barak was too timid to rise to the occasion unless Deborah accompanied him. She agreed, but told him that though he might have the victory, a woman would be credited with actually killing Sisera.

As the enemy readied for war against Israel, Deborah gave instructions to Barak: "'Up! For this *is* the day in which the Lord has delivered Sisera into your hand. Has not the Lord gone out before you?' So Barak went down from Mount Tabor with ten thousand men following him. And the Lord routed Sisera and all *his* chariots and all *his* army with the edge of the sword before Barak; and Sisera alighted from *his* chariot and fled away on foot" (Judges 4:14–15).

Warrior and Military Strategist

Deborah heeded Barak and went with him to Kedesh, where he rallied the men of Naphtali and Zebulun, two of the twelve sons of Israel. He set out with an army of ten thousand men, with Deborah at his side. Sisera had nine hundred chariots of iron with a great army of men, but could not overcome the paltry Israelite army.

Deborah was a strategist. The weather forecast was favorable to Israel that day, and she made full use of it. "Deborah tricked the over-confident enemy into driving their iron-wheeled chariots onto marshy land where they were bogged down. Then the Israelite slingsmen and archers picked them off one by one. The enemy forces were routed, their troops slaughtered, and the Israelites were jubilant."[1]

As referenced by Deen, historically, there has been a small

---

[1] Elizabeth Fletcher, *Women in the Bible*: Deborah and Jael, 2006, accessed May 30, 2015, http://www.womeninthebible.net/women-bible-old-new-testaments/deborah-and-jael/.

number of women who have ever achieved the supreme authority and public dignity of Deborah the judge. She lived about thirteen centuries before Jesus Christ, in the era of the judges, and was the only woman in the Bible who served her country, by the collective voice of the people, at the height of their political power. Deen compares Deborah to Joan of Arc, who ably led the French army to victory twenty-seven centuries later.

Lockyer describes Deborah as a wife, a prophetess, an agitator, a ruler, a warrior, a poetess, a maternal figure, and a fearless patriot. Deborah was also a counselor. Most of all, she was a woman of great faith who rose to the occasion to victoriously lead her people, not only as a warrior, but as a judge for many years.

Ancient belief categorizes the bee as among the highest in intelligence in the animal kingdom, says Mary Hallet. This is backed by scientific proof. Thomas D. Seeley, in his book *Honeybee Democracy*, discusses the collective intelligence of a multitude of bees working in harmony to create a team, with abilities far transcending those of its constituents. He focuses on how a swarm of honeybees, when choosing its home, makes democratic decisions through a form of collective intelligence.[2]

Since the name Deborah means *bee*, it is appropriate that she is among the wisest of all the women in the Old Testament. With Deborah at his side, Barak and his army decimated Jabin and his superior Canaanite army. But Sisera escaped and ran for his life. Or so he thought. God's Word had already gone forth, revealed to His prophetess, Deborah.

Jael

Sisera was on good terms with the house of Heber the Kenite, and ran to the tent of Heber's wife, Jael. She went out to meet him and invited him to turn aside into her tent. She was very hospitable. She covered him with a blanket. He asked for water, and she gave him milk. He asked her to stand watch at the door

---

[2] Thomas Seeley, *Honeybee Democracy* (Princeton, NJ: Princeton University Press, 2010).

and, if anyone inquired about him, to say there was no man there. She complied with his wishes. Then the enemy fell asleep, and as apprehensive as she might have been, Jael sprang into action.

The Song of Deborah tells the story:

> She stretched her hand to the tent peg,
> Her right hand to the workmen's hammer;
> She pounded Sisera, she pierced his head,
> She split and struck through his temple.
> At her feet he sank, he fell, he lay still;
> At her feet he sank, he fell;
> Where he sank, there he fell dead. (Judg. 5:26–27)

Sisera's mother anxiously awaited his return, all in vain.

Viewpoint

It was not by power, not by might, but by the Spirit of God that the victory came to Israel. Deborah knew that if God was on her side, she could not fail, no matter how fierce the enemy seemed or what superior arms they possessed. As a matter of fact, God had already told her to prophesy to Barak that he would have the victory over Sisera that day. It was God's appointed time for the battle.

Barak, though cowardly, was obedient to the servant of God. He mustered his troops and went out to battle under Deborah's command. If God was on their side, who could be against them? She was able to encourage the Israelite army to press on, regardless of the equipment they lacked, the size of their army, or the weather conditions. It took great faith to go forward. Deborah had enough to go around.

Jael, the wife of Heber the Kenite, was able to lure Sisera into her tent because of the good relations her husband had with him. God already knew how He was going to deliver His people from oppression by the enemy. He knew the victory that day was with the women.

Both Deborah and Jael must be commended, because without the latter, the enemy would have lived to fight Israel another day. Lockyer argues that Jael acted treacherously and will forever be held accountable for the brutal way she killed Sisera. Wesley takes this view: "Probably Jael at that time intended him no other than kindness, 'till God by an immediate impulse on her mind, directed her to do otherwise."[3]

Deborah in her song praised Jael for the tremendous part she played that day:

> "Most blessed among women is Jael,
> The wife of Heber the Kenite;
> Blessed is she among women in tents." (Judg. 5:24).

But we are warned, "The eulogy must be considered as pronounced not on the moral character of the woman and her deed, but on the public benefits which, in the overruling providence of God, would flow from it."[4] Again, God can use anyone and any means to fulfill His will.

Deborah in the New Testament

Although she is not mentioned by name, Deborah's faith is implicitly praised by reference to Barak in the New Testament:

> And what more shall I say? For the time would fail me to tell of Gideon and Barak and Samson and Jephthah, also of David and Samuel and the

---

[3] John Wesley, *Wesley's Notes on the Bible: The Old Testament* (Port Richey, FL: NTS Library, n. d.), http://ntslibrary.com/PDF%20Books/Wesley's%20Notes%20on%20the%20Bible.pdf, 945.

[4] Robert Jamieson, A. R. Fausset, and David Brown, *Commentary Critical and Explanatory on the Whole Bible: The Old Testament* (Grand Rapids, MI: Christian Classics Ethereal Library, n. d.), http://www.ccel.org/ccel/jamieson/jfb.x.vii.iv.html, Judges, chapter 4, Judg. 4:21.

prophets: who through faith subdued kingdoms, worked righteousness, obtained promises, stopped the mouths of lions, quenched the violence of fire, escaped the edge of the sword, out of weakness were made strong, became valiant in battle, turned to flight the armies of the aliens. (Heb. 11:32–34)

One could question why Deborah's name was not included here by Paul. She did not hesitate as Barak did, but moved on faith. She was the brilliant one encouraging Barak and his men not to look at the situation or the size of Sisera's army, but to God, the Author and Finisher of their faith. Whether Paul neglected Deborah by oversight or design, one will never know.

Barak's victory came that day, not primarily from him, but from the woman, Deborah the judge, whose ears were attuned to the Word of God. She proved she was about her Father's business, and had enough faith for herself and the entire army of Israel.

CHAPTER 9

RUTH, THE MOABITESS (CIRCA 1125 BC)

Loyalty Displayed

During the time when Israel was ruled by judges, there was a severe famine in the land of Judah. Elimelech, a Bethlehemite, took his wife Noami and two sons, Mahlon and Chilion, and moved to Moab. Their sons married Moabite women: Mahlon married Ruth, and Chilion married Orpah. Unfortunately, all three husbands died. Their wives, now widows, had no choice but to provide for themselves.

Ruth, the Moabitess, is introduced to us as a humble, loyal, industrious, generous, modest, courteous, and loving young woman. Her mother-in-law, Naomi, widowed and bereaved of her two sons, told Ruth and Orpah to return to their homes. She was leaving for Bethlehem, because she received good news that the famine in her homeland, which had driven her family to Moab, was now over. Ruth and Orpah, crying, followed her, but Orpah soon went her own way, never to be heard of again.

Ruth, on the other hand, would not turn back. She was persistent, though encouraged by Naomi to follow her sister-in-law and go back to her own people and gods. Ruth would not let Naomi out of her sight. Naomi said she was too old to bear any more sons. This did not deter Ruth. Ruth had a made-up mind, and replied to her mother-in-law with one of the greatest speeches written in the Bible:

> "Entreat me not to leave you,
> *Or to* turn back from following after you;
> For wherever you go, I will go;
> And wherever you lodge, I will lodge;
> Your people *shall be* my people,
> And your God, my God.
> Where you die, I will die,
> And there will I be buried.
> The Lᴏʀᴅ do so to me, and more also,
> If *anything but* death parts you and me." (Ruth 1:16–17)

This is the speech of a pagan woman, a Moabite, whom the Jews were forbidden to marry. Ruth claimed not only Naomi's people, but more importantly, the God she served, the true and living God.

The Bible says you must believe in your heart and confess with your tongue that Jesus Christ is Lord. Ruth unknowingly was doing just that, for "in the beginning was the Word, and the Word was with God, and the Word was God" (John 1:1). She was under the protection of God from the moment her confession of faith was uttered.

Mother, Daughter, and Barley Season

After those words, Naomi stopped trying to influence Ruth. They made their way to Bethlehem together, just as barley season was starting. Naomi changed her speech. She no longer called Ruth daughter-in-law, but daughter. Ruth asked to go to the fields and glean barley, and Naomi gave her consent. The field where Ruth elected to glean belonged to Boaz. He was an older, prominent citizen, and a close relative of Naomi's dead husband.

Favor

Boaz was a wealthy man. When he visited the reapers in his field, he saw Ruth and asked who she was. He learned that she was Naomi's daughter-in-law who had sought permission to glean among the sheaves. "So she came and has continued from morning until now, though she rested a little in the house" (Ruth 2:7). Ruth received a good report from the reapers.

Boaz cautioned Ruth to stay close to his reapers:

> You will listen, my daughter, will you not? Do not go to glean in another field, nor go from here, but stay close by my young women. *Let* your eyes *be* on the field which they reap, and go after them. Have I not commanded the young men not to touch you? And when you are thirsty, go to the vessels and drink from what the young men have drawn. (Ruth 2:8–9)

Ruth was filled with humility and gratitude and "fell on her face, bowed down to the ground and said to Boaz, 'Why have I found favor in your eyes, that you should take notice of me, since I *am* a foreigner?'" (Ruth 2:10). Ruth was not aware that her light was shining brightly, and many had taken notice of her faithfulness and industriousness. Boaz was attracted to Ruth for two reasons: because of her beauty and also because of her personality. He had heard people talking and was positively impacted by what was said.

Boaz replied:

> It has been fully reported to me, all that you have done for your mother-in-law since the death of your husband, and *how* you have left your father

and your mother and the land of your birth, and have come to a people whom you did not know before. The Lord repay your work, and a full reward be given you by the Lord God of Israel, under whose wings you have come for refuge. (Ruth 2:11–12)

Ruth never lost sight of who she was. She thanked Boaz for the comfort and favor he had bestowed upon her, even though she was a foreigner, and not like one of his maidservants. Boaz gave her the main reason she was so favored: she had come under the wings of the God of Israel for refuge, and He is faithful. It is written:

> He who dwells in the secret place of the Most High
> Shall abide under the shadow of the Almighty.
> I will say of the Lord, "He is my refuge and my fortress;
> My God in Him will I trust." (Ps. 91:1–2)

Ruth was now in that place of refuge, under the full anointing and protection of God. God chose Boaz to be the one to shower Ruth with His blessings.

At mealtime, Ruth was invited to eat with the other workers and dip her bread in the vinegar. She ate till she was full, but kept some back. Ruth had her new mother on her mind.

She returned to her gleaning, and even more favor was given. "Boaz commanded his young men, saying, 'Let her glean even among the sheaves, and do not reproach her. Also let *grain* from the bundles fall purposely for her; leave *it* that she may glean, and do not rebuke her'" (Ruth 2:15–16). No tongue was to rise up against Ruth, and no weapon was to be formed against her.

Women were very vulnerable when out in the fields. It was easy for them to be physically and emotionally exploited by male reapers. Ruth, young, good-looking, and a stranger, was a prime target. But it was her season to be favored by God. Boaz particularly cautioned his workmen not to be abusive to her, and he asked them to make sure they left extra grain behind for her to glean.

By evening, Ruth had gleaned about an ephah, or a bushel, of barley and took it home. First, Naomi was given the bread Ruth had kept back from lunch. Then, Naomi, like any good mother, wanted a full report of how Ruth had spent the day and where she had gleaned. She added, "Blessed be the one who took notice of you" (Ruth 2:19). Naomi learned that this person was Boaz, her dead husband's relative, and exclaimed, "Blessed *be* he of the LORD, who has not forsaken His kindness to the living and the dead!" And Naomi said to her, "This man *is* a relation of ours, one of our close relatives" (Ruth 2:20).

Naomi told Ruth, "*It is* good, my daughter, that you go out with his young women, and that people do not meet you in any other field" (Ruth 2:22).

Ruth continued to go to Boaz's field until the end of barley season. Then Naomi decided it was time to find security for her daughter by seeking a husband for her.

Lessons for Success

Naomi gave Ruth very specific instructions about what to do:

1. Wash and anoint yourself, put on your best garment, and go down to the threshing floor.
2. Do not make yourself known to Boaz until he has finished eating and drinking.
3. When he lies down, notice the place where he lies. Go in, uncover his feet, and lie down. (See Ruth 3:3–4)

Once Ruth followed these instructions, Naomi told her, "[Boaz] will tell you what you should do" (Ruth 3:4). And dutifully Ruth responded, "All that you say to me I will do" (Ruth 3:5). She followed to the letter.

Boaz ate and drank to his heart's content, and was in a very cheerful mood when he went to lie down at the end of a heap of grain. He promptly fell asleep. Obediently, Ruth uncovered his feet and quietly lay down. This was not an act of impropriety on the part of Ruth, states Jamieson et al., but a reminder to Boaz that he was her dead husband's relative, and therefore had a responsibility to perform. It was permissible in the culture of that time for a servant to lie crosswise at his master's feet and share his covering. Also, creating the sensation of cool air on his feet was a way to purposely wake him from his slumber.

At midnight, Boaz awoke, astounded to discover a woman, not only on the threshing floor, but lying at his feet. "Who are you?" he asked.

And Ruth replied, "I *am* Ruth, your maidservant. Take your maidservant under your wing, for you are a close relative" (Ruth 3:9). Talk about women's liberation and tenacity!

Boaz responded, "Blessed *are* you of the LORD, my daughter! For you have shown more kindness at the end than at the beginning, in that you did not go after young men, whether poor or rich. And now, my daughter, do not fear. I will do for you all that you request, for all the people of my town know that you *are* a virtuous woman" (Ruth 3:10–11).

"Who can find a virtuous wife?" (Prov. 31:10). Ruth proved to be such a woman, far above rubies. Boaz called her "daughter" because he was an older man and was honored to know that Ruth, though young, had chosen him over any of the many young men she had met.

God is a God of order. There was another kinsman, an even closer relative, who had the right to redeem Ruth. Boaz, as fortunate as he may have felt to have Ruth choose him, knew he had to do what was right, but promised if this other relative would not execute the duty, he would be absolutely delighted to comply. This was the same duty Onan had been called on to do for Tamar, his brother's wife: marry her and raise up children to his dead brother. But Onan refused to comply.

Ruth, always obedient, followed Boaz's instructions to stay at his feet until morning. She did not want it made public that she had come to the threshing floor, so she arose early to leave. Boaz said to her, "'Bring the shawl that *is* on you and hold it.' And when she held it, he measured six *ephahs* of barley, and laid *it* on her. Then she went into the city" (Ruth 3:15). He did not want her going empty-handed to her mother.

Ruth must have been bursting with joy and expectation as she hurried home to Naomi to relate all the events of the night. Naomi's quick lessons had yielded fruit for her daughter. Naomi continued her advice to Ruth: "Sit still, my daughter, until you know how the matter will turn out; for the man will not rest until he has concluded the matter this day" (Ruth 3:18).

Man of His Word

Boaz did not procrastinate. He found the other close relative and gathered ten of the elders of the city as witnesses. He told the other relative all about Ruth, the Moabitess, and their duty to redeem the land that Naomi had sold, which had belonged to her husband, Elimelech. In fact, by this time the land belonged not only to Naomi, but also to Ruth and Orpah, but the latter had already forfeited her claim by remaining in Moab.

Boaz told him there was no other but the two of them to redeem the sold land. The near kinsman agreed to help redeem the land, but he did not know the stipulations that would follow. Boaz surprised him: "On the day you buy the field from the hand of Naomi, you must also buy *it* from Ruth the Moabitess, the wife of the dead, to perpetuate the name of the dead through his inheritance" (Ruth 4:5).

The relative had thought it was just a matter of redeeming some land: "I will redeem it" (Ruth 4:4). But what was this other matter? Taking a Moabitess as wife? Give up his own inheritance for the sake of a dead man? Not at all! He told Boaz, "I cannot redeem *it* for myself, lest I ruin my own inheritance. You redeem my right of redemption for yourself, for I cannot redeem *it*" (Ruth 4:60). The Bible account says the close relative followed the custom of taking off his sandal and giving it to Boaz to confirm that his intention was to pass it on.

Boaz spoke to the witnesses he had assembled, saying that all the land that had been Naomi's, Chilion's, and Mahlon's, he now bought from Naomi. And he kept the best for last: "Moreover, Ruth the Moabitess, the widow of Mahlon, I have acquired as my wife, to perpetuate the name of the dead through his inheritance, that the name of the dead may not be cut off from among his brethren and from his position at the gate. You *are* witnesses this day" (Ruth 4:10).

Blessings were called on Boaz and Ruth from the elders and all the people at the city gate:

> The LORD make the woman who is coming to your house like Rachel and Leah, the two who built the house of Israel; and may you prosper in Ephrathah and be famous in Bethlehem. May your house be like the house of Perez, whom Tamar bore to Judah, because of the offspring which the LORD will give you from this young woman. (Ruth 4:11–12)

Ruth married Boaz and bore him a son, the joy of Naomi's old age. His name was Obed, the father of Jesse the Bethlehemite, who was the father of David.

Viewpoint

Like many immigrants and migrants, Ruth left Moab to seek a better life with her mother-in-law. Not everyone meets with the success that she did. She was young, widowed, and childless when she arrived in Bethlehem. Though the famine was over, she and Naomi had to provide for themselves—as is the fate of many widows if their husbands do not leave them financially secure.

Ruth was not afraid of work. She asked that Naomi allow her to go to the fields to glean, since it was the beginning of barley season. She became the breadwinner for them both, and was overwhelmingly excited to be so. Her conscientiousness did not go unnoticed by the reapers or by Boaz, a close relative of her dead husband, Mahlon, and the wealthy owner of the fields where she gleaned.

When Ruth left Moab, she left her world behind. She made up her mind to serve the true and living God that Naomi served. There was no turning back. She put her hand to the plough, and there was no ambivalence in her, as there had been in Orpah. The Bible tells us that a double-minded person is unstable in all his ways, and so gets nothing in return. Ruth's determination was evident from the very outset, and paid off handsomely for her. Her resolve not to let Naomi out of her sight brings to mind Elisha, who refused to turn back from following Elijah. Determination paid off for him too. He got his heart's desire—a double portion of Elijah's anointing.

But it was more than just a made-up mind. It was mainly Ruth's confession of the living God, plus a combination of her willingness to be obedient to Naomi and Boaz, humility, hard work, and faithfulness that brought her such great success in a strange land. When we serve God faithfully, He leads us in the path of righteousness. Ruth made the God of Naomi her God, and that is all God requires—that you confess Him with your tongue and believe in your heart that He is God, the God of all possibilities.

Ruth, whose name means *a friend*, learned what it meant to have her cup running over, to have a Friend who sticks closer than a brother. She, a Gentile woman, whose ancestral roots were embedded in incest, received more than a double portion of blessings. She had the honor of becoming the great-grandmother of David, highly venerated; a major link in the bloodline of Jesus Christ, our Lord and Savior; and an excellent example to young women everywhere.

Many are called but few are chosen. The near kinsman had the first choice to marry Ruth, but declined when he realized the responsibility that came with it. Many young men are not up to the task of shouldering responsibility. Boaz, whose name means *strength*, was chosen over the near kinsman, who, like Orpah, could not make up his mind. Those of us who fall into this category are wimpy Christians, selfish, and unstable in all our ways. We end up missing out on our blessings.

The covenant was already made with Jesus, the Second Person of the Trinity, and God knew who would be included in the genealogy of His Son. He was laying the foundation. Strength and wisdom prevailed. Bishop Hall says, "Boaz, instead of touching her as a wanton, blesseth her as a father, encourages her as a friend, promises her as a kinsman, rewards her as a patron, and sends her away laden with hopes and gifts, no less chast[e], but more happy than she came."[1]

Though Ruth came to the threshing floor, Boaz treated her with the utmost kindness and respect. He fulfilled his promise to her the very same day, settling the matter as to who would marry her. Ruth's reward was sure because she left all behind: "Everyone who has left houses or brothers or sisters or father or mother or wife or children or lands, for My name's sake, shall receive a hundredfold, and inherit eternal life" (Matt. 19:29). This is the Word of God.

Ruth gleaned the very best in the fields, and even more from God, because she never looked back at the Egypt she left behind. She trusted God, the Author and Finisher of her faith, to direct her path. She acknowledged Him in all her ways, under the adept guidance of Naomi, whose bitterness was turned to pure joy.

Only when we unconditionally set out to follow Jesus will we reap His choicest blessings. Ruth did. She, Boaz, and Naomi, along with all their friends and well-wishers, in their delight and joy, had no foreknowledge of how exceedingly special the child Obed was. "Obed begot Jesse, and Jesse begot David" (Ruth 4:22). Jesus Christ came from David, with whom God personally made an eternal covenant—that his throne would be established forever.

---

[1] John Wesley, *Wesley's Notes on the Bible*: *The Old Testament* (Port Richey, FL: NTS Library, n. d.), http://ntslibrary.com/PDF%20Books/Wesley's%20Notes%20on%20the%20Bible.pdf, 979.

CHAPTER 10

HANNAH
(CIRCA 1110 BC)

Taunted but Loved

Hannah was the wife of Elkanah the Ephraimite, and she was barren. Hannah longed to have a child, but the Lord had shut up her womb. To make matters worse, Elkanah took a second wife, Peninnah, by whom he had children. Peninnah taunted Hannah because of her inability to have children, and Hannah was sorely grieved.

Each year, the family went on a pilgrimage to Shiloh, to sacrifice to and worship the Lord of Hosts. Year by year, Hannah wept and did not eat because of Peninnah's provocation. But Elkanah loved Hannah. "Whenever the time came for Elkanah to make an offering, he would give portions to Peninnah his wife and to all her sons and daughters. But to Hannah he would give a double portion, for he loved Hannah, although the LORD had closed her womb" (1 Sam. 1:4–5).

He spoke kindly to her and tried to comfort her: "Why is your heart grieved? Am I not better to you than ten sons?" (1 Sam. 1:8). Maybe so, but as a man, he could not fully identify with Hannah's need, so deeply rooted and so unfulfilled. To him it did not seem like a big deal, because he had children by Peninnah. He loved Hannah anyway. As Sam Keen says, love isn't finding a perfect person. It's seeing an imperfect person perfectly. Elkanah did not care about Hannah's imperfection. It is the same way our Maker, our Creator, looks beyond our faults and our imperfections every day of our lives, loving us anyway.

Hannah never doubted that she was loved, but there were some things Elkanah did not understand. She was a woman, longing to cradle her own child and rock him on her breast. Like Tamar, she wanted to experience motherhood for herself. She could not be comforted by her husband, so she went to the tabernacle, sought solace in prayer, and made her request known to God.

Prayer Request

> And she *was* in bitterness of soul, and prayed to the Lord and wept in anguish. Then she made a vow and said, "O Lord of hosts, if You will indeed look on the affliction of Your maidservant and remember me, and not forget Your maidservant, but will give Your maidservant a male child, then I will give him to the Lord all the days of his life, and no razor shall come upon his head." (1 Sam. 1:10–11)

Eli the priest was sitting near the doorpost of the Lord's tabernacle, and saw Hannah in prayer. Thinking she was intoxicated, he asked her how long she would continue her drinking and urged her to put her wine away. But an anguished reply came from the very depths of her being:

> No, my lord, I *am* a woman of sorrowful spirit. I have drunk neither wine nor intoxicating drink, but have poured out my soul before the Lord. Do not consider your maidservant a wicked woman, for out of the abundance of my complaint and grief I have spoken until now. (1 Sam. 1:15–16)

What Eli was witnessing was the outpouring of many years of abject longing, of anguish, of tears, of hoping for a child; only her lips moved, but her heart was overwhelmed with sorrow, and "Hannah spoke in her heart." Out of the abundance of the heart, the issues of life come, and the mouth speaks. Eli blessed her and wished that God would grant her heart's desire.

God truly looks at the heart, and Hannah's heart was pure before Him. She had offered her double portion of offerings to Him. She was encouraged and comforted and "went her way and ate, and her face was no longer *sad*," because she had an expectation and a hope.

Prayer Answered

Early next day, they worshipped before the Lord, then made their journey back to Ramah, and "Elkanah knew Hannah his wife, and the LORD remembered her" (1 Sam. 1:19). Hannah conceived. A son was born to her and she called him Samuel, "*saying, 'Because I have asked for him from the LORD'*" (1 Sam. 1:20).

Another year passed, and it was time for their annual pilgrimage to Shiloh. Elkanah and his entire household made preparations to go, but Hannah declined. She told her husband she would not go up until Samuel was weaned: "Then I will take him, that he may appear before the LORD and remain there forever" (1 Sam. 1:22). Elkanah told her do what she felt was right, "Only let the LORD establish His Word" (1 Sam. 1:23).

Offering, Worship, and Thanksgiving

Hannah nursed the child she had so desired. Her joy must have been unspeakable. But she had to fulfill a vow, a covenant she had made with the Lord. When Samuel was weaned, she made that journey to Shiloh, taking her child and the necessary offerings: three bulls, a skin of wine, and an ephah of flour. She went to Eli the priest and said:

> O my lord! As your soul lives, my lord, I *am* the woman who stood by you here, praying to the LORD. For this child I prayed, and the LORD has granted me my petition which I asked of Him. Therefore I also have lent him to the LORD; as long as he lives he shall be lent to the LORD. (1 Sam. 1:26–28)

And the Bible says they worshipped there.

Elkanah was the high priest of his home and led his household in the things of God. He knew the value of worship: "This man went up from his city yearly to worship and sacrifice to the LORD of hosts in Shiloh" (1 Sam. 1:3). We were made to worship the Most High God, and we must worship Him in spirit and in truth. The Father is seeking such to worship Him (John 4:23–24). Even as Hannah was about to give up the son she loved so dearly, the family bowed in worship and Hannah prayed:

> "My heart rejoices in the LORD;
> My horn is exalted in the LORD.
> I smile at my enemies,
> Because I rejoice in Your salvation." (1 Sam. 2:1)

> "Talk no more so very proudly;
> Let no arrogance come from your mouth,
> For the LORD *is* the God of knowledge;
> And by Him actions are weighed." (1 Sam. 2:3)

Her prayer came from a heart that was full of joy, gratitude, and satisfaction. God had taken away her shame. She no longer had to put up with Peninnah's arrogance. There is a song that states, "Blessed is the child that has his own." Hannah finally knew what it felt like having her own child. Her horn was greatly exalted.

The family went back to Ramah, but Samuel stayed in Shiloh under Eli's care, ministering to the Lord. Every year when Hannah went up to Shiloh, she made a new garment for her son. Once a mother, always a mother, and a mother's love never runs dry.

Viewpoint

God blessed Hannah, and she bore more children. God brought her from a place of bitterness and need to a place of extreme joy and no lack. God is not moved by our needs, because He already knows what we have need of from day to day. Hannah's need was great in her eyes, but nothing for the God who opened the Red Sea and the Jordan River for His people, so they could cross over on dry ground. The faith she put into action with good works was recompensed to her.

When Eli told her to go in peace and wished that God might grant her petition, her response was, "Let your maidservant find favor in your sight." She did not complain or argue, but in faith accepted his blessing. She immediately changed her disposition and waited upon the Lord, who showed favor indeed to her. The Lord opened Hannah's womb.

We hear of babies born and abandoned, time and time again—unwanted babies, they are called. For every unwanted pregnancy, there is a woman somewhere who is desperately hoping to become pregnant. Only a barren woman, with formerly no hope of bearing a child, can truly identify with the Sarahs, Rebekahs, Rachels, and Hannahs of this world. What exquisite joy they finally experience!

There is a true, modern-day story of a woman, Ann Pettway, who wanted a child. But every time she became pregnant, she miscarried or gave birth to a dead baby. She longed to take her own little newborn home from the hospital, but she always awoke to empty arms. So great was her desire to birth a child that she decided to try again.

Her doctor assured her that everything was all right, and this baby would be fine. She was ecstatic. Finally the day of delivery came, and this tortured soul awoke to the same tragic end: empty arms.

Then she devised a plan to go to the hospital and steal a baby. She took a baby girl. For many years, she brought the girl up as her own, showering her with all the love she could.

Finally, though, the truth came out. Today Ann Pettway is

incarcerated, sentenced to twelve years in 2012 for her crime of kidnapping baby White in 1987. Carlina White was nineteen days old when she disappeared from the hospital without a trace. Her parents lived through a real horror when the police could find no evidence of their firstborn. One can hardly imagine the pain caused to them by the loss of their child.

But can you identify with the pain of disappointment after disappointment that Pettway endured? One can easily sympathize with rather than blame this woman for her crime. The story was made into a television movie: *Abducted: The Carlina White Story*.

Perhaps what was missing from Ann Pettway's life was faith in God. From the way her story unfolded, it seems Ann existed purely in the physical realm, often strung out on drugs. As a child, she had been emotionally and physically abused, beaten with extension cords and belts by her mother. She suffered from acute depression due to the many miscarriages and stillbirths.

She had faith enough to try again for a child, but her faith was in the doctor. Did she believe that God could bring her through that pregnancy? Our faith must be rooted and grounded in Jesus Christ, for vain is the help of man. Did she go before God and make supplication like Hannah did? Did she even know the power of prayer, or that God is the same yesterday, today, and forever, the worker of all miracles? We know God hears and answers prayers, and His Word says to ask and we shall receive. The outcome was so very different for Hannah than for Pettway.

But Pettway must have kept asking. She must have been secretly crying out to God. For in 1998, Ann birthed a son and raised him as Carlina's brother. God finally granted her wish.

It did not obliterate the crime she had committed. That shadow was looming in the distance. When the story finally broke, on the day of sentencing, she apologized to Carlina's parents: "I am here today to right my wrong and ask for forgiveness."

Hannah, whose name means *favor* or *grace*, asked and waited in faith. Her disappointment and sorrow turned into happiness. Thank God for His grace and His favor. Hannah prayed specifically for a boy child, and she never forgot her promise, her vow, to return him to the Lord.

Many of us, when we find ourselves in situations, make all kinds of promises to God, but once we obtain His favor, we forget even to say thank you. Time and time again, we go back on our vows. The Word of God says it is better not to vow, than to vow and not pay, because when our calamity comes, God will laugh.

A person should adhere to his or her word. Hannah kept her part of the covenant, and Samuel grew up before the Lord to be one of the great, gifted prophets of the Old Testament. He was the last judge of Israel, anointed both Saul and David as kings of Israel, and was instrumental in spiritually turning the people back to God.

Hannah in the New Testament

Hannah is not mentioned by name in the New Testament and is not a part of the bloodline of Jesus Christ. But His mother Mary's song in the gospel of Luke, the Magnificat as it is called in Latin, is modeled on Hannah's song (see Luke 1:46–55; compare 1 Sam. 2:1–10). The notes on Hannah's song in the King James Study Bible state,

> Hannah's prayer is a song of praise and thanksgiving to God ... This song has sometimes been termed the "Magnificat of the OT" because it is so similar to the Magnificat of the NT ... Hannah speaks prophetically at a time when Israel is about to enter an important new period of her history with the establishment of kingship through her son, Samuel ... The supreme source of Hannah's joy is not in the child, but in the God who has answered her prayer ... To have one's horn lifted up by God is to be delivered from disgrace to a position of honor and strength.

CHAPTER 11

ABIGAIL (CIRCA 1014 BC)

Disrespect From a Scoundrel

Abigail was the wife of Nabal, a very rich but miserly individual. She was "a woman of good understanding and beautiful appearance" (1 Sam. 25:3). Nabal was sheep shearing in Carmel, and king designate David heard of it. He was hiding in the mountains with six hundred of his followers because King Saul sought his life. On a feast day, he sent ten of his young men to Nabal:

> Go up to Carmel, go to Nabal, and greet him in my name. And thus you shall say to him who lives *in prosperity:* "Peace *be* to you, peace to your house, and peace to all that you have! Now I have heard that you have shearers. Your shepherds were with us, and we did not hurt them, nor was there anything missing from them all the while they were in Carmel." (1 Sam. 25:5–7)

David felt that since Nabal's shepherds had been protected by his young men, he would be favored. "Therefore let *my* young men find favor in your eyes, for we come on a feast day. Please give whatever comes to your hand to your servant and to your son David" (v. 8).

Such a gracious request on a feast day was blatantly refused by Nabal. "Who *is* David, and who *is* the son of Jesse? There are many servants nowadays who break away each one from his master. Shall I then take my bread and my water and my meat that I have killed for my shearers, and give *it* to men when I do not know where they *are* from?" (1 Sam. 25:10–11).

The name Nabal means *fool*. Nabal proved he was out of the loop. He was ignorant of who David was and that his shepherds had been protected by David's men. Certainly, he had no fear of the Lord.

> The fear of the Lord *is* the beginning of knowledge,
> *But* fools despise wisdom and instruction. (Prov. 1:7)

David's men returned and told him how Nabal had reacted. David was outraged. He purposed in his heart to destroy Nabal and all the men of his household that very night.

But one of Nabal's servants told Abigail, his wife, what had transpired between her husband and David's men. "For he is *such* a scoundrel that one cannot speak to him" (1 Sam. 25:17).

She Came Bearing Gifts

Immediately Abigail prepared and loaded a feast fit for a king, and sent her servants before her as she went to meet David and his men. When she encountered them, she dismounted from her donkey, bowed to the ground, and fell on her face at his feet, begging David not to go forward with his plan to destroy her household. She persuaded him to accept the present she had brought for his young men, and not shed blood without a cause or seek his own revenge.

> Then David said to Abigail: "Blessed *is* the LORD
> God of Israel, who sent you this day to meet me!
> And blessed *is* your advice and blessed *are* you,
> because you have kept me this day from coming
> to bloodshed and from avenging myself with my
> own hand. For indeed, *as* the LORD God of Israel
> lives, who has kept me back from hurting you,
> unless you had hurried and come to meet me,
> surely by morning light no males would have
> been left to Nabal!" (1 Sam. 25:32–34)

When Abigail returned to her home, she found her husband feasting and very drunk, so she said nothing to him that night. When he was sober next day, she informed him what had transpired with David. The Word of God says Nabal's heart died within him, and he became as a stone. After ten days, he died, struck by the Lord. No longer could he execute any authority over all he had proclaimed was his. His bread, water, meat, and riches were about to go to a man more worthy than him.

David heard about Nabal's demise. He sent a proposal to Abigail, and made her his wife.

Wisdom Prevails

Abigail was a woman of wisdom. She realized that if she did nothing in response to the folly of her husband, the bloodshed and destruction intended for her household would undoubtedly take place. She was a woman who took care of her household. She explained to David that she had had no knowledge his young men had come to her husband. Her maturity, wisdom, and understanding were evident when she loaded those donkeys and hastened to meet her king.

She prophesied to him that he would survive Saul's assaults, but he would taint his monarchy if he went forward with his plan against Nabal that night. David recognized she was blessed, and the advice she gave was exactly what he needed to hear at that moment.

In a very short space of time thereafter, her prudence won her the most envied position of her time: the wife of the king, the anointed of God.

> What but the unquestioning faith in God could have dictated such a humble petition? In it Abigail typifies woman in her noblest, purest character. Her actions reveal that she was a diplomat of the highest order and that she understood men and had tolerance for their bad behavior.[1]

Viewpoint

Wisdom and humility—what a fantastic combination! Abigail was such a woman, created and fully endowed by God for the mission she so ably accomplished—saving His anointed, David, from committing willful sin and destroying her household. Lockyer describes her as having beauty and brains. A woman of beauty with as beautiful a mind as she had was definitely one of God's masterpieces.

The book of Proverbs recommends in all of your getting, get understanding, and the beginning of knowledge is fear of the Lord. Understanding and wisdom are what prevailed when this woman of God moved on faith and hastened to correct the wrong of her idiotic husband. She can be numbered among the peacemakers:

> "Blessed *are* the peacemakers,
> For they shall be called the sons of God." (Matt. 5:9)

---

[1] Edith Deen, *All of the Women of the Bible* (San Francisco: HarperCollins, 1955), 104.

According to Jamieson et al.,

> Dismounting in presence of a superior is the highest token of respect that can be given; and it is still an essential act of homage to the great. Accompanying this act of courtesy with the lowest form of prostration, she not only by her attitude, but her language, made the fullest amends for the disrespect shown by her husband, as well as paid the fullest tribute of respect to the character and claims of David.[2]

Abigail's quick thinking and actions saved not only her household, but helped David to keep his legacy from being tarnished. "'Vengeance is Mine, I will repay,' says the Lord" (Heb. 10:30). David was about to take matters into his own hands and become a law unto himself, acting out of the will of God. Abigail's sound counsel averted such a crisis. King of Israel that he was destined to be, David had to admit that Abigail's advice was blessed, and she was blessed for giving it. His proposal to her proved how much he respected and admired her, and was a token of his sincere gratitude that God had used her to stop him from folly.

As a Hebrew woman, Lockyer explains, Abigail was constrained by the customs of her day. She was only able to give counsel in times of greatest emergency. In going to David, Abigail did not act irrationally, but palpably risked the wrath of her own husband, whose life was in danger.

Beauty is said to be in the eye of the beholder. An individual can be beautiful inside, outside, or both. In the world, we encounter many beautiful women, but not all of them demonstrate the capacity for wisdom. Abigail did not approach her drunken husband before she left or after she returned. She knew there

---

[2] Robert Jamieson, A. R. Fausset, and David Brown, *Commentary Critical and Explanatory on the Whole Bible* (Grand Rapids, MI: Christian Classic Ethereal Library, n. d.), http://www.ccel.org/ccel/jamieson/jfb.x.ix.xxv.html, 1 Sam. 25:23.

was no reasoning or understanding that could transpire between her and an inebriated fool. Nabal had so much, he did not miss the provisions his wife had taken to David and his men, until she informed him the next day.

Abigail knew the kind of man her husband was, but never complained. She was a woman of God. Only love could have made her risk alienating her husband, and infuriating her king even more by attempting to give him womanly advice.

The Bible states that all things work together for good to them that love the Lord. God moves in mysterious ways, and who can question Him? Nabal dropped dead ten days later. God not only kept His servant David from evil, but also avenged him of Nabal's reproach.

Abigail, a gracious, wise, and patient woman, was loosed from the bonds of a wearisome marriage and free to accept the proposal of her king, which she did in all humility. "But he who is greatest among you shall be your servant" (Matt. 23:11). Abigail presented herself as a maidservant, ready to wash the feet of her lord's servants, when David's messengers brought his request for her hand in marriage.

Countless women are in marriages that are as frustrating as Abigail's was, yet try to hold fast to their vows. Some endure horrific physical abuse, for many drunken husbands are wife beaters. Other women are so embarrassed about their marital issues, they shun counsel from their spiritual leaders or those qualified to assist. Rather, they suffer in silence. Some have lost their lives trying to escape abusive relationships.

Centers for battered women and children are full to capacity, and exist because these ills persist in our society. Sad to say, statistics show that several pastors and men of the cloth fall into the category of abusers.

Lockyer suggests that though Abigail's life was miserable, and she may have been beaten, insulted, and spurned during Nabal's bouts of drinking, she remained faithful to the man she had married. There are many women who choose to continue in abusive relationships in the name of love. Others continue mainly out of fear of their mate or of the unknown, especially when children are involved. Some stay because they are committed to the vows they made before God. Someone humorously stated you get married sixteen times—four richer, four poorer, four better, and four worse. Abigail had no children then, and the Bible does not state she was physically abused by Nabal, but life could not have been very pleasant for her.

As she stood faithful to her first husband, so she remained faithful to King David throughout his persecution by Saul, until her prophetic words came to pass and David was fully vested as Israel's great king. She bore David a son, Chileab.

One day, while David and his men were out fighting the Philistines, the Amalekites struck David's camp in Ziklag, capturing Abigail, David's second wife Ahinoam, all the children, and all the supplies. David received a positive response when he inquired of God whether he should pursue the perpetrators. He and four hundred of his men followed, attacked the Amalekites, and rescued Abigail, Ahinoam, and the children. They also recovered all that the Amalekites had taken from Judah in Ziklag, just as the Lord had spoken.

Abigail in the New Testament

Abigail's name means *father,* or *leader of the dance,* or *leader of joy.* She is one of the great women of faith, though not mentioned in the New Testament. She brought stability and wealth to David when he was most in need. There is a proverb that says behind every great man, there is a great woman. This was Abigail to King David, the man after God's own heart. David was able to discern the heart of Abigail and accept her God-given counsel on a night when the only things on his mind were revenge and bloodshed.

CHAPTER 12

JEZEBEL (CIRCA 874 BC)

Ill-Fated Marriage

King Ahab took Jezebel, the daughter of Ethbaal, king of the Sidonians, to be his wife. The Sidonians were worshippers of Baal, and possibly to impress his new wife, Ahab built an altar to Baal. This was exactly what the Lord God commanded he should not do—thou shalt not have any strange gods before Me. Jezebel, whose name means *the whore of Baal*, was a very domineering woman and strongly influenced her husband.

In the Bible, each king is presented as being more evil than those before him. But of them all, Towns agrees, the one presented as the most evil and diabolical of all was the son and successor of Omri, King Ahab. Scripture plainly describes his behavior: "Now Ahab the son of Omri did evil in the sight of the Lord, more than all who were before him" (1 Kings 16:30). "But there was no one like Ahab, who sold himself to do wickedness in the sight of the Lord, because Jezebel his wife stirred him up. And he behaved very abominably in following idols, according to all that the Amorites had done, whom the Lord had cast out before the children of Israel" (1 Kings 21:25–26).

Jezebel had the power to stir up Ahab. She had no idea that

God was raising up one of His greatest prophets of all time, and one who was no pushover: Elijah the Tishbite. He prophesied a drought. As he told Ahab, there would not be dew or rain during those years, except at his word.

Drought and Vengeance

Elijah's words came to pass. Ahab and Jezebel were furious. As the drought and famine increased, the search for Elijah intensified. Jezebel began to kill off the prophets of God one by one, and many had to hide to save their lives. But Elijah was the one the evil king and his queen sought the most. At this time, God sent Elijah to the widow woman in Zarephath, a city which was ruled by Jezebel's father.

When God was ready to bring the drought to an end, He told Elijah to present himself to Ahab. Although the man of God knew that his life was in jeopardy with wicked Ahab and Jezebel, he was obedient and sent Obadiah, Ahab's trusted servant and a prophet himself, to seek his master. Obadiah, because of his fear of the Lord, had hidden a hundred prophets and fed them water and bread. In so doing, he saved them from the senseless massacre Jezebel was waging.

Obadiah was skeptical of Elijah's order. Elijah promised him he would not disappear. Elijah was serious about meeting Ahab that very day.

Ahab called him a troubler of Israel. Elijah retorted, "I have not troubled Israel, but you and your father's house *have,* in that you have forsaken the commandments of the Lord and have followed the Baals" (1 Kings 18:18).

True Power

Ahab sent for all Israel and the prophets to come to Mount Carmel. Elijah spoke to the people. "How long will you falter between two opinions? If the Lord *is* God, follow Him; but if Baal, follow him" (1 Kings 18:21). Then Elijah had a miraculous victory from the Lord over the prophets of Baal.

He made a proposal: both he and the prophets of Baal would prepare a bull sacrifice. "You call on the name of your gods, and I will call on the name of the LORD; and the God who answers by fire, He is God" (1 Kings 18:24). The prophets of Baal pleaded, leaped around, prophesied, and cut themselves until their blood gushed out, but no answer came. Their sacrifice was never consumed.

The man of God proved his God by building a trench around the altar, filling it with water, and saturating his sacrifice with water three times over. Yet it was consumed by fire from heaven for all the people to see. Then Elijah commanded that all the false prophets of Baal be caught and killed.

The king told Jezebel that Elijah had orchestrated the death of four hundred prophets of Baal. She was incensed. "Then Jezebel sent a messenger to Elijah, saying, 'So let the gods do *to me,* and more also, if I do not make your life as the life of one of them by tomorrow about this time'" (1 Kings 19:2).

Elijah was not taking any chances at all with Jezebel; he ran for his life. Rightly so! Jezebel operated as though she were a law unto herself and vengeance was hers.

Abusive Power

Naboth and his sons experienced Jezebel's full wrath when Naboth refused to sell his vineyard to covetous Ahab. Naboth was a Jezreelite who possessed a vineyard in Jezreel, adjacent to Ahab's palace in Samaria. Ahab was all about self. He approached Naboth. "Give me your vineyard, that I may have it for a vegetable garden, because it *is* near, next to my house; and for it I will give you a vineyard better than it. *Or,* if it seems good to you, I will give you its worth in money" (1 Kings 21:2).

Naboth replied: "The LORD forbid that I should give the inheritance of my fathers to you" (1 Kings 21:3).

Used to getting his own selfish way all the time, Ahab went away sullen and would not eat. His dear wife, Jezebel, inquired about his welfare. He explained about Naboth, the Jezreelite, and Naboth's refusal to sell him his inheritance. "Then Jezebel his wife said to him, 'You now exercise authority over Israel! Arise, eat food, and let your heart be cheerful; I will give you the vineyard of Naboth the Jezreelite'" (1 Kings 21:7).

Jezebel was in all her twisted glory, and began devising her devious scheme to take Naboth's vineyard for her husband. The Bible tells us she wrote letters in the king's name, used his seal, and sent them to the nobles and elders who lived in the city with Naboth. Her message to them was "Proclaim a fast, and seat Naboth with high honor among the people; and seat two men, scoundrels, before him to bear witness against him, saying, 'You have blasphemed God and the king.' *Then* take him out, and stone him, that he may die" (1 Kings 21:9–10).

When this criminal act of willful murder was completed, word was sent to Jezebel that Naboth had been stoned to death. On receiving the news, she told Ahab to arise and take possession of the vineyard that he had been refused, because Naboth was no longer. Gleefully, Ahab obeyed his treacherous wife.

But the Word of God came from the prophet that the dogs would lick his blood in the same place they licked Naboth's. There was also a message for Queen Jezebel from the Lord: "And concerning Jezebel the LORD also spoke, saying, 'The dogs shall eat Jezebel by the wall of Jezreel. The dogs shall eat whoever belongs to Ahab and dies in the city, and the birds of the air shall eat whoever dies in the field'" (1 Kings 21:23–24).

Ahab humbled himself, and God relented for the time being, bringing the calamity in the days of his son instead. But with Jezebel, there was no contrition for all the harlotries and witchcraft she had committed as queen. God set His plan in order to accomplish what He had said: that all the house of Ahab should perish.

Jehu was anointed king of Israel. God's Word came to him to eradicate the house of Ahab, and fulfill the prediction that the dogs would eat Jezebel "on the plot *of ground* at Jezreel and *there shall be* none to bury *her*" (2 Kings 9:10).

God's Word Accomplished

When Jehu came to Jezreel,

> Jezebel heard *of it;* and she put paint on her eyes
> and adorned her head, and looked through a
> window. Then, as Jehu entered at the gate, she
> said, *"Is it* peace, Zimri, murderer of your master?"
> And he looked up at the window, and said, "Who
> *is* on my side? Who?" So two *or* three eunuchs
> looked out at him. Then he said, "Throw her
> down." So they threw her down, and *some* of her
> blood spattered on the wall and on the horses;
> and he trampled her underfoot. (2 Kings 9:30–33)

Violence begets violence. Jezebel's end was as violent as her life. But she was a king's daughter, and Jehu commanded, "'Go now, see to this accursed *woman,* and bury her, for she was a king's daughter.' So they went to bury her, but they found no more of her than the skull and the feet and the palms of *her* hands" (2 Kings 9: 34–35). They came and reported this to Jehu, who answered, "This *is* the word of the LORD, which He spoke by His servant Elijah the Tishbite, saying, 'On the plot *of ground* at Jezreel dogs shall eat the flesh of Jezebel and the corpse of Jezebel shall be as refuse on the surface of the field, in the plot at Jezreel, so that they shall not say, "Here *lies* Jezebel"'" (2 Kings 9:36–37).

Viewpoint

Evil always destroys itself. The psalmist says, "Fret not thyself because of evil doers" (Ps. 37:1). Elijah did not even wait to confront the evil that Jezebel had planned for him. He took off and found himself in a cave, "in the secret place of the Most High." He knew she was capable of fulfilling her threat, and he could not face such wickedness on his own.

Jezebel's heart was demonic, intent on evil, and she did whatever it took to get her own way. Revenge was rooted in her heart, and all the issues of life come out of the heart. Even the Almighty, our Creator, stated that the heart of man is wicked continually.

Jezebel did not care if the innocent paid with their very lives. She killed God's prophets and took pleasure in doing so. But the Lord instructs,

> "Do not touch My anointed ones,
> And do My prophets no harm." (1 Chron. 16:22)

He meant exactly that.

David understood this principle when he came upon Saul, his enemy, fast asleep in a cave. He took his spear and cut a small piece of Saul's garment, but even that minute act troubled him very much. He knew that Saul was the anointed of God, and David, even though the kingdom was taken from Saul and given to him, always respected and honored Saul as king, even in death.

Ahab and Jezebel were extremely wicked, but Ahab humbled himself and asked forgiveness. God promised, because of his humility, that He would spare him seeing the destruction of his household in his lifetime, but his son would inherit it. The sins of the parents fall many times upon the children. Jezebel and his son came to that violent end.

> The Word of God *is* living and powerful, and sharper than any two-edged sword, piercing even to the division of soul and spirit, and of joints and marrow, and is a discerner of the thoughts and intents of the heart. And there is no creature hidden from His sight, but all things *are* naked and open to the eyes of Him to whom we *must give* account. (Heb. 4:12–13)

Nothing is hidden from God. Whatever we do in this life, we must give a full account to God. What God intends will prevail. He is absolute Authority. Sometimes the evil is so great that God says it has come up to His nostrils, and He has to do something about it. This happened in the case of Sodom and Gomorrah—sudden destruction. And that is what Jezebel came to, because of the evil intent of her heart that was naked before God.

God's Word says to live at peace with all men. He promised that if our ways please Him, He will make even our enemies to be at peace with us. If we know God, then we know peace, but if there is no God, there is no peace.

Jezebel was powerful, strong-willed, determined to defy anyone and anything, and wicked in all her ways. She thrived on evil, and it was her undoing. She demonstrated callousness even to the innocent, and that was what the eunuchs returned to her at Jehu's command, "Throw her down." King's daughter or not, God is no respecter of any person.

The deliberate use of power to harm does not make for greatness. Power must be tempered with discipline and used in a responsible manner. Temperance is one of the fruits of the Spirit. There are women who are domineering and egocentric, characteristics typical of Jezebel. They may think that they are so compelling, nothing can stand in their paths. There is no fear of God in them.

But ultimately, like Jezebel, they should fear what God can do. He is the only Authority none can challenge, and definitively, the only Authority that matters. He will always have a remnant, even two or three eunuchs, to answer the call and accomplish His will.

Jezebel in the New Testament

Jezebel is mentioned in conjunction with the corruption in one of the seven churches, the church in Thyatira. When the Romans exiled John to the small, desolate island of Patmos, God sent His angel to reveal to him things that would soon take place, which John was ordered to write and send to the seven churches in Asia: Ephesus, Smyrna, Pergamos, Thyatira, Sardis, Philadelphia, and Laodicea.

"And to the angel of the church in Thyatira write, 'These things says the Son of God, who has eyes like a flame of fire, and His feet like fine brass: 'I know your works, love, service, faith, and your patience ... Nevertheless I have a few things against you, because you allow that woman Jezebel, who calls herself a prophetess, to teach and seduce My servants to commit sexual immorality and eat things sacrificed to idols. And I gave her time to repent of her sexual immorality, and she did not repent. Indeed I will cast her into a sickbed, and those who commit adultery with her into great tribulation, unless they repent of their deeds. I will kill her children with death, and all the churches shall know that I am He who searches the minds and hearts. And I will give to each one of you according to your works.'" (Rev. 2:18, 20–23)

Jezebel the queen, a self-proclaimed prophetess, led Ahab down the wrong path. In the very same way, a woman named Jezebel, in the church in Thyatira, claimed to be a prophetess. Many mistakenly attributed her powers to God, and were being led astray. A true prophetess is not self-proclaimed. God is the one who empowers, "not he who commends himself is approved, but whom the Lord commends" (2 Cor. 10:18).

The church in Thyatira would be called to account for violating God's instruction that women were not allowed to teach or preach in the church, and for permitting this woman Jezebel not only to teach, but to teach wrong doctrine. Women were permitted to teach other women and children. The roles of men and women in the church were and are designated by God.

CHAPTER 13

ESTHER (CIRCA 479 BC)

Deposing a Queen

Vashti, queen of Persia, refused to appear before her husband, King Ahasuerus, on the seventh day of a huge banquet held at the royal court. Vashti was beautiful, and the king felt like showing off his queen to his court, but she would not come. This angered King Ahasuerus greatly, and in his semi-intoxicated state, he acted rashly by accepting the advice of his personal servants. Vashti was deposed, and a nationwide hunt began for a new queen. It is at this point we meet Esther, the Hebrew maiden.

Esther the Virgin

Born Hadassah, meaning *myrtle*, the girl also known as Esther, meaning *star*, was orphaned and grew up with her cousin Mordecai. Young, beautiful, and a virgin, she fit the profile of the beautiful young virgins the king's men were seeking as candidates for queen. "A nation-wide search for a new queen began – the first recorded beauty contest in the world. A young Jewess was among the candidates. Her beauty was so extraordinary that she 'pleased' even the chief eunuch Hegai, who had been castrated while still a young boy."[1]

Esther was part of the diaspora of Jews who did not return to Judah after the Babylonian exile. After seventy years, many Jews felt at home in Babylon and opted to remain there.

Esther was among the maidens chosen to replace Queen Vashti. The name Esther also means *hidden*—her Jewish ancestry was kept a secret. Mordecai cautioned her not to reveal her identity. The young virgins had a one-year preparation period before they could go before the king. Esther followed the instructions of Hegai very closely, since he knew the king's tastes.

> Now when the turn came for Esther ... to go in to the king, she requested nothing but what Hegai the king's eunuch, the custodian of the women, advised. And Esther obtained favor in the sight of all who saw her ... The king loved Esther more than all the *other* women, and she obtained grace and favor in his sight more than all the virgins; so he set the royal crown upon her head and made her queen instead of Vashti. (Esther 2:15–17)

As the virgins gathered a second time, Mordecai was sitting at the king's gate and overheard a plot by two of the doorkeepers to destroy the king. Mordecai informed Esther, who made the matter known to King Ahasuerus, in her cousin's name. The two doorkeepers were immediately punished by hanging, and the incident was recorded in the presence of the king, in the book of the chronicles.

Haman, one of the king's servants, received a promotion from his master, King Ahasuerus. He was now above all the other princes, and everyone paid him homage, including those who

---

[1] Elizabeth Fletcher, *Women in the Bible: Esther, Queen, Bible Woman*, 2006, accessed June 8, 2015, http://www.womeninthebible.net/women-bible-old-new-testaments/esther-her-story/, The Search for a Beautiful Virgin.

were within the king's gate. That is, all except Mordecai, the Jew, who resolutely refused to do so.

Chosen for a Reason

The Bible says the devil is always there to steal our joy. No sooner had Esther become queen of Persia than trouble began to brew. Haman, angry that Mordecai would not bow to him, decided not only to eliminate Mordecai, but to extinguish all the Jews. He went to the king for permission to execute the plan he had hatched:

> "There is a certain people scattered and dispersed among the people in all the provinces of your kingdom; their laws *are* different from all *other* people's, and they do not keep the king's laws. Therefore it *is* not fitting for the king to let them remain. If it pleases the king, let *a decree* be written that they be destroyed." (Esther 3:8–9)

At that time, Haman was in the king's favor. Ahasuerus gave Haman the royal signet ring and all the financial resources necessary for the success of his mission.

In the provinces, everyone received a letter in his or her own language, "to destroy, to kill, and to annihilate all the Jews," whether old, young, women, or children, on the thirteenth day of the twelfth month. After reading the decree, the people of Shushan were bewildered. Shushan is a city of Elam, located on the River Ulai. It was the administrative capital of the Persian empire, and the place where King Ahasuerus held court.

Grief-stricken, Mordecai put on sackcloth and ashes, symbols of mourning, and "cried out with a loud and bitter cry" in the city, and all the way up to the king's front gate, for he could not go within dressed in sackcloth. He was not alone: "In every province where the king's command and decree arrived, *there was* great mourning among the Jews, with fasting, weeping, and wailing; and many lay in sackcloth and ashes" (Esther 4:3).

A Time to Fast

Esther was informed by her maids and eunuchs about Mordecai. Deeply grieved, she sent garments to him so he could change, but he would not. She sent to inquire the reason for her cousin's distress, and learned it was all because of Haman's wicked plan to fill the king's coffers by annihilating the Jews. In addition, Mordecai gave Hathach, Esther's eunuch, a copy of the decree written for their destruction, and instructions she should go to King Ahasuerus and plead the cause of her people.

Esther sent a message back to Mordecai: going before the king, without being summoned, would be disastrous for her. The king's law stated that all would be put to death except one to whom he held out the golden scepter. Esther had not been called by Ahasuerus for the last thirty days. Matthew Henry explains that this was a very foolish law that made even the king quite unhappy. It had been made not for his safety, but to flatter his pride. Access to him was difficult and infrequent, so when he was finally seen, he was revered as a little god.

Mordecai returned the answer that Esther should not think she would escape death because she was in the king's palace. "For if you remain completely silent at this time, relief and deliverance will arise for the Jews from another place, but you and your father's house will perish. Yet who knows whether you have come to the kingdom for *such* a time as this?" (Esther 4:14).

Esther's courageous reply was "Go, gather all the Jews who are present in Shushan, and fast for me; neither eat nor drink for three days, night or day. My maids and I will fast likewise. And so I will go to the king, which *is* against the law; and if I perish, I perish!" (Esther 4:16)

What we call the Esther Fast was inaugurated as she requested, and Esther embarked upon the mission at hand.

Favor and an Invitation

She went into the court dressed in her royal attire, and when the king saw her, "she found favor in his sight." He held out the royal scepter and offered to give up to half his kingdom to fulfill her request. She asked the king and Haman to come to a banquet she was preparing that day. The king agreed and urged Haman to be quick to do as Esther had asked.

Again at the banquet, the king reiterated his offer of up to half his kingdom to satisfy Esther's petition. Esther extended another invitation: if she had found favor in the king's sight, would he and Haman again come to the banquet she would prepare on the morrow? Then she would make her petition known.

The king and Haman complied. After the king repeated his offer a third time, Esther finally spoke:

> "If I have found favor in your sight, O king, and if it pleases the king, let my life be given me at my petition, and my people at my request. For we have been sold, my people and I, to be destroyed, to be killed, and to be annihilated. Had we been sold as male and female slaves, I would have held my tongue, although the enemy could never compensate for the king's loss." (Esther 7:3–4)

An outraged king demanded to know who would dare do such a thing. Esther said it was "this wicked Haman!"

Victory

Indignant, King Ahasuerus decreed Haman should be hanged on the gallows he had built for Mordecai. Haman's house was given to Esther that very day. She appealed to Ahasuerus to revoke the letters Haman had sent, and save her people. She and Mordecai received permission to write their own decree in the king's name, sealed with his ring, to counter Haman's.

Esther had secured the freedom of her people throughout the provinces. "And in every province and city, wherever the king's command and decree came, the Jews had joy and gladness, a feast and a holiday. Then many of the people of the land became Jews, because fear of the Jews fell upon them" (Esther 8:17).

The Jews were God's chosen people. He chose them when He brought them out of the land of Egypt after 430 years of suffering. He did not bring them thus far to leave them forsaken. Esther was the chosen vessel to redeem her people, even as our heavenly Father chose His beloved Son to redeem the world after the fall of Adam.

Viewpoint

Everyone is born for a special purpose. If we wait upon God, He will reveal that purpose. In a preview to the book of Esther, the New King James Version declares, "God's Hand of providence and protection on behalf of His people is evident throughout the book of Esther, though His Name does not appear once." Mordecai said, "Yet who knows whether you have come to the kingdom for such a time as this?" (Esther 4:14).

Though she was still quite young, it was Esther's time to rise up and be courageous. Deen describes her as a woman who, besides being devoted to the cause of her people, demonstrated genuine faith and high courage. God, who is faithful, always provides for His children in their hour of need.

As Mordecai expressed it, if Esther had been reluctant to take action, God would have sent salvation by some other means. He sent Moses to Pharaoh, who eventually had to let His people go. David, quite a young lad, was not afraid of the mighty giant Goliath, whom he brought down with a sling and a stone. In the days of the judges, God sent Gideon, Ehud, Othniel, and Deborah, among others. He sent His prophets Isaiah, Elijah, Elisha, Samuel, and a host of others. God always hears the cry of His people and rescues them from their dilemma—at times in most miraculous ways. Last but not least, He sent His only begotten Son, Jesus

Christ, in whom salvation is free to all, and who constantly hears our cries and our groaning.

At this time, the entire nation of the Jews was crying out to God. Often we hear the expression, "It's who you know." Most of the Jews felt helpless, but Mordecai knew they had someone on the inside: Esther, his young cousin. He knew Esther had won the heart of the king, so he employed her aid.

Time was short, but when the occasion demanded swift action, Esther embraced the danger. She did not fear for her safety, but acted for the greater good of her people. Jesus told His disciples that sometimes the answer will not come except by prayer and fasting. This mission was crucial, so Esther instituted a three-day dry fast.

When God gives hard choices, it is as a test of faith and obedience to His will. It was important for Esther to remember her roots and work on behalf of her people. She learned that God does not deny His children when they walk in His righteousness. He gives favor to them, even as He told Moses: "I will have mercy on whomever I will have mercy, and I will have compassion on whomever I will have compassion" (Rom. 9:15).

Using skill and wisdom, Esther tactfully addressed the situation with her husband to achieve the reversal of Haman's notorious plot to annihilate her people. She invited Ahasuerus to two banquets, making sure firstly that he was at ease, and secondly that she had truly gained his favor. Her star shone very brightly.

We may not be called to save a nation or anything so great, but in our daily walk, we encounter opportunities to do exceptional things, allowing our light to shine as we look beyond self and embrace the will of God. We should always utilize these precious occasions.

This is what Esther did. She made sure she prepared thoroughly through prayer and fasting. She unquestionably was not only clothed in her royal attire, but in the anointing power of God, under the divine guidance of the Holy Spirit. Queen Esther sought the King of Kings before she approached her husband, the king of Persia.

As believers, we should be spiritually prepared in every

circumstance, as Esther was. Very often we seek solutions to our problems, forgetting that, regardless of the situation, there is a duality, physical and spiritual, of which we must be cognizant. Frequently we forget the spiritual.

Seek God first, in every situation. Be clothed in the full armor of God and walk in His might. He is amazing.

Esther in the New Testament

Esther is not mentioned in the New Testament, but she lives on in the hearts and minds of the Jews, who celebrate the feast of Purim annually, on the fourteenth and fifteenth of March, the month of Adar, when God favored them and saved a nation from annihilation.

> Mordecai wrote these things and sent letters to all the Jews ... to establish among them that they should celebrate yearly the fourteenth and fifteenth days of the month of Adar, as the days on which the Jews had rest from their enemies, as the month which was turned from sorrow to joy for them, and from mourning to a holiday; that they should make them days of feasting and joy, of sending presents to one another and gifts to the poor ... *that* these days *should be* remembered and kept throughout every generation, every family, every province, and every city, that these days of Purim should not fail *to be observed* among the Jews, and *that* the memory of them should not perish among their descendants. Then Queen Esther, the daughter of Abihail, with Mordecai the Jew, wrote with full authority to confirm this second letter about Purim ... So the decree of Esther confirmed these matters of Purim, and it was written in the book. (Esther 9:20–22, 28–29, 32)

CHAPTER 14

ELIZABETH
(FIRST CENTURY BC)

A Prophecy Fulfilled

Elizabeth, meaning *God her oath*, was mother of John the Baptist and wife of Zacharias, a priest. Luke introduces Elizabeth as follows:

> There was in the days of Herod, the king of Judea, a certain priest named Zacharias, of the division of Abijah. His wife *was* of the daughters of Aaron, and her name *was* Elizabeth. And they were both righteous before God, walking in all the commandments and ordinances of the Lord blameless. But they had no child, because Elizabeth was barren, and they were both well advanced in years. (Luke 1:5–7)

Immediately we are told that Elizabeth was a righteous woman walking blamelessly before God. So was her husband. The problem with this remarkable couple was that they were childless and elderly. Elizabeth was barren, and though that condition

112

for a woman was a great embarrassment in her day, she never gave up faith in God. She was not just the wife of a priest, but also the daughter of one. Lockyer states that barrenness was humiliating because every Jewish woman fantasized about having the privilege of being the mother of the Messiah, promised to Eve, earth's first mother. "And I will put enmity between you and the woman, and between your seed and her Seed; He shall bruise your head, and you shall bruise His heel" (Gen. 3:15). Jamieson et al., note that "thy seed" refers not only to evil spirits, but to wicked men. "Seed of the woman" refers to the Messiah, or His church.

When Zacharias received the good news that he and his wife would finally have a son, his response to the Angel Gabriel was doubt: he and his wife were too advanced in years. For his unbelief, he was struck dumb until the prophecy was fulfilled.

Elizabeth conceived as was foretold and hid herself for five months, reflecting, "Thus the Lord has dealt with me, in the days when He looked on *me*, to take away my reproach among people" (Luke 1:25). Elizabeth stayed out of the public eye until her pregnancy was evident to all.

At the baby's circumcision, all expected the child to be called by his father's name, as was the custom. But Elizabeth said he was to be called John. Zacharias corroborated this when he wrote on a tablet, "His name is John." Immediately, miraculously, Zacharias was able to speak again. He had communicated to his wife the angel's prophecy and the name designated for their son—most likely by writing, as he had done before everyone else. Elizabeth was in total accord with her husband.

The Visit and Salutation

In her sixth month of pregnancy, Elizabeth was paid a special visit by her young cousin Mary. The Angel Gabriel was pretty busy visiting the people of God to tell them the great news God had sent him to deliver. He also visited Mary, who found out that Elizabeth was with child. Mary hastened to a city of Judah, in the hill country, to inquire after Elizabeth's well-being.

Mary had likewise been told the most astounding news about herself: she had been chosen, among all women, to be the mother of the Christ. As Mary greeted her cousin, Elizabeth was filled with the Holy Spirit and spontaneously exclaimed:

> "Blessed *are* you among women, and blessed *is* the fruit of your womb! But why *is* this *granted* to me, that the mother of my Lord should come to me? For indeed, as soon as the voice of your greeting sounded in my ears, the babe leaped in my womb for joy. Blessed *is* she who believed, for there will be a fulfillment of those things which were told her from the Lord." (Luke 1:42–45)

Amazingly, the Baptist, yet unborn, paid homage to his unborn King. His mother, without any prompting, proclaimed the fruit still in Mary's womb as her Lord. Such involuntary proclamation could only be inspired by the Holy Spirit.

> What beautiful superiority to *envy* have we here! High as was the distinction conferred upon herself, Elisabeth loses sight of it altogether, in presence of one more honored still; upon whom, with her unborn Babe, in an ecstasy of inspiration, she pronounces a benediction, feeling it to be a wonder unaccountable that "the mother of her Lord should come to *her*."[1]

Viewpoint

Like Sarah and Abraham, Elizabeth and Zacharias had grown old together and had not had a child. Whereas God Himself communed with Abraham, the Angel Gabriel brought the tidings

---

[1] Robert Jamieson, A. R. Fausset, and David Brown, *Commentary Critical and Explanatory on the Whole Bible* (Grand Rapids, MI: Christian Classic Ethereal Library, n. d.), http://www.ccel.org/ccel/jamieson/jfb.i.html, Luke 1:42-44.

of great joy to Zacharias: he and his wife would finally have a son, John. Abraham Kuyper mentions Elizabeth was "the last sapling to spring from the soil of Aaron's house, who fulfilled the holy vocation which God called that family to fulfill. Judah was to give birth to the Messiah, but Aaron was to worship Him in service."[2]

Elizabeth did not show herself for five months. When Mary visited her, she was in her sixth month of pregnancy. She felt her child leap in her womb, and she returned Mary's salutation with a powerful, profound salutation of her own that could only have come from the inspiration of the Holy Ghost.

As God did with Sarah, so He did with Elizabeth. Four hundred years had passed since the voice of the last prophet, Malachi, was heard in Israel. The Jews knew the Messiah was coming, but had no idea how or when. But He who knows all and sees all was about to fulfill His promise to Eve. Elizabeth was told, through her husband, that the child in her womb was special. Since the Messiah was coming with no fanfare, His cousin John, just about five months His senior, would be His herald, the forerunner to point the people to Him. "Behold! The Lamb of God who takes away the sin of the world" (John 1:29). Jesus told the multitude: "This is *he* of whom it is written:

> 'Behold, I send My messenger before Your face,
> Who will prepare Your way before You.'

> For I say to you, among those born of women there is not a greater prophet than John the Baptist; but he who is least in the kingdom of God is greater than he." (Luke 7:27–28)

Elizabeth accomplished the purpose God had established for her life when she was far advanced in age. Her spiritual walk

---

[2] Abraham Kuyper, *Women of the New Testament: 30 Devotional Messages for Women's Groups* (Grand Rapids, MI: Zondervan, 1934), 8.

made her worthy of becoming the mother of the precursor of Jesus Christ, our Lord and Savior.

Zacharias was dumb, and as Wesley mentions, the verb used in the original text indicates he was also deaf, because they had to make signs to him. Because of this, Elizabeth could have agreed with all those who desired her to follow tradition and name the child after his father. She could have gone against her husband's wishes and succumbed to the pressure to choose a traditional family name, since no relative had ever been called by the name John. She did not. When Zacharias was consulted, he agreed with his wife.

Those present were shocked. The Bible says the two shall become one. It didn't matter that for over nine months, her husband had been unable to hear or speak. This aged couple had been walking together for a long time, and found a way to communicate with each other. Zacharias made sure his wife understood the importance of the child she had conceived. After all, he had been struck dumb because of his unbelief. God had conferred a special blessing on the fruit of her womb; this was no ordinary child she was carrying. The last step in sealing the blessing was to call the child's name John. As soon as this last instruction of Gabriel was accomplished, Zacharias received his healing.

There are times we have to break away from tradition. God's will takes priority. When we shut out the noise, humble ourselves, and submit to the Most High, we experience the blessings and miracles God has in store for us. The only thing He requires is our complete obedience to Him.

Elizabeth is a great example of Paul's precept: "Wives, submit to your own husbands, as to the Lord. For the husband is head of the wife, as also Christ is head of the church; and He is the Savior of the body. Therefore, just as the church is subject to Christ, so *let* the wives *be* to their own husbands in everything" (Eph. 5:22–24). She did not let anyone intervene in the final decision between them.

It is a lesson that many wives would do well to follow, allowing husbands to freely perform their God-given roles as high priest of their homes. Some wives try, as the saying goes, to wear both the pants and the dress. Single mothers are forced into such a position. But when husband and wife reside together, God has certainly conferred headship to the husband: "I want you to know that the head of every man is Christ, the head of woman is man, and the head of Christ is God" (1 Cor. 11:3).

Elizabeth is only mentioned in the book of Luke, chapter 1, in the New Testament.

CHAPTER 15

THE VIRGIN MARY
(15 BC TO AD 48)

Promise of Old

From the time Adam and Eve sinned, God promised to send a Redeemer, One who would be able to reconcile us back to Him. The Bible unequivocally states God is not a man that He should lie. Immutability is one of His attributes; He does not change. In the fullness of time, He sent His only begotten Son, that whoever believes in Him should not perish but have everlasting life. This promise from John 3:16 is the most famous and quoted statement from John, the beloved disciple.

How would God accomplish this promise? "Therefore the Lord Himself will give you a sign: Behold, the virgin shall conceive and bear a Son, and shall call His name Immanuel," which means *God is with us* (Isa. 7:14).

Good News

Mary, a young virgin engaged to a man named Joseph, was a descendent of David. Miriam, meaning *their rebellion*, is the

Hebrew version of the name Mary. Matthew gives the genealogy of Jesus through Joseph, whose father was clearly stated to be Jacob (Matt. 1:16). Luke also gives the genealogy of Jesus, stating that Joseph was the son of Heli. "Son of" means *son-in-law* of Heli, since the genealogies are customarily given through the fathers. Therefore, Luke 3:23–38 traces Mary's genealogy all the way back to Adam, the son of God.

Mary received a visit from the Angel Gabriel, who had an unusual greeting: "Rejoice, highly favored *one,* the Lord *is* with you; blessed *are* you among women" (Luke 1:28). Mary was disturbed, but:

> The angel said to her, "Do not be afraid, Mary, for you have found favor with God. And behold, you will conceive in your womb and bring forth a Son, and shall call His name JESUS. He will be great, and will be called the Son of the Highest; and the Lord God will give Him the throne of His father David. And He will reign over the house of Jacob forever, and of His kingdom there will be no end." (Luke 1:30–33)

Mary was told she would conceive of the Holy Ghost, and the Child would be called the Son of God. Also, her cousin Elizabeth was with child, no longer barren, for with God, nothing is impossible. Mary responded, "Behold the maidservant of the Lord! Let it be to me according to your word" (Luke 1:38). Mary pondered these things in her heart as she hastened to visit her elderly cousin.

As the Angel Gabriel had greeted Mary, so did Elizabeth—as blessed among women. John the Baptist, in his sixth month of gestation, leaped in his mother's womb. She proclaimed herself not worthy that her cousin Mary, mother of her Lord, should come to her. This confirmed what Gabriel had said, though confirmation was not necessary, since Mary had fully acquiesced to the will of God.

Mary spent three months with Elizabeth, then returned to

Nazareth of Galilee to her betrothed, Joseph. She had some explaining to do. She had asked the angel, "How can this be, since I do not know a man?" She trusted the angel's reassurance—but Joseph had not heard the angel. How could she explain her pregnancy to him, since their marriage was not yet consummated?

Joseph thought of putting her aside secretly, so she would not be shamed. Matthew records that an angel then spoke to Joseph in a dream, reassuring him not to be afraid to take Mary as his wife. The angel revealed the identity of the Child and that His name would be called Jesus. He was destined to save His people from their sins. Joseph heeded the instructions and cared for Mary.

A Time to Be Born

As the time drew near for Mary to birth her Son, Caesar Augustus, the first Roman emperor, called for a census. Joseph had to go to Bethlehem because he was a descendant of the house of David. He took Mary with him to be registered as his wife. After a long and arduous journey, they arrived in Bethlehem.

Mary realized the birth of her Son was imminent. Her husband sought a place for her to deliver her Baby, only to find all the inns were full. All of the house of David had journeyed to Bethlehem to fulfill Augustus's decree.

This was unfortunate for Mary. Every woman who has ever given birth knows that when the crucial hour is at hand, time is of the essence. Joseph understood he had to do something to help his wife.

He found a stable, and Mary "brought forth her firstborn Son, and wrapped Him in swaddling cloths, and laid Him in a manger, because there was no room for them in the inn" (Luke 2:7). Ironically, there was no room for the King of Kings, Possessor of all things, the One to whom the earth and all its fullness belong. There was no room for the Lord of Lords, the only begotten Son of the Father.

Saving the Savior

When Herod learned that a young king had been born in Bethlehem of Judea, he cunningly tried to learn His whereabouts from the wise men of the East, who had seen His star and come to pay homage. But the Father was able to protect His Son, and again sent an angel to Joseph in a dream. The angel instructed Joseph to take his family and flee to Egypt, because evil was intended by Herod against the Child.

By now, Joseph knew how important his role was and hastened to obey. The family remained in Egypt until further instructions were forthcoming. Mary never complained, but followed her husband's directives. Certainly, she would have heard of Herod's violence against the innocents—male children, two years of age and under, were slaughtered in Bethlehem to ensure the young king would not survive.

When it was safe, an angel again directed them in a dream to return. Joseph took his family to Nazareth of Galilee, where he and Mary nurtured their Son. We next hear of the family when Jesus was twelve years of age and they went to Jerusalem to celebrate the Passover.

> When they had finished the days, as they returned, the Boy Jesus lingered behind in Jerusalem. And Joseph and His mother did not know *it;* but supposing Him to have been in the company, they went a day's journey, and sought Him among *their* relatives and acquaintances. So when they did not find Him, they returned to Jerusalem, seeking Him. Now so it was *that* after three days they found Him in the temple, sitting in the midst of the teachers, both listening to them and asking them questions. And all who heard Him were astonished at His understanding and answers. So when they saw Him, they were amazed; and His mother said to Him, "Son, why have You done this to us? Look, Your father and

I have sought You anxiously." And He said to them, "Why did you seek Me? Did you not know that I must be about My Father's business?" But they did not understand the statement which He spoke to them. (Luke 2:43-50)

As always, her heart was open to understanding. Mary pondered these things.

When Mary requested His intervention at the marriage feast at Cana of Galilee, she did not worry about Jesus's initial rebuke. She had no doubt that Jesus would respond positively, because of that special bond between mother and son.

Heartbreak and Desolation

Little did Mary know or imagine the horrific turn of events that would end Jesus's earthly life three short years later, after His first miracle of turning water into wine at Cana . Helplessly, Mary stood by from a distance and saw her firstborn Son convicted, beaten, spat upon, ridiculed, crowned with thorns, insulted, condemned, and made to carry the very cross to which He was nailed on Calvary. Maybe then she understood the implication of Simeon's prophecy, made when Jesus was circumcised: "Yes, a sword will pierce through your own soul also." She had no idea how deeply! Jamieson et al., comment on Luke 2:35:

> "Blessed as thou art among women, thou shalt have thine own deep share of the struggles and sufferings which this Babe is to occasion"— pointing not only to the continued obloquy and rejection of this Child of hers, those agonies of His which she was to witness at the cross, and her desolate condition thereafter, but to dreadful alternations of faith and unbelief, of hope and

fear regarding Him, which she would have to pass through.[1]

Viewpoint

Young Virgin Mary was given the great news that, of all the fair maidens in the land of Israel, she was the fairest of all. She received the coveted news from the Angel Gabriel that she had been chosen to be the mother of the Redeemer. In and through her, God was finally bringing His Word to fulfillment. He had made His promise to Adam and Eve, and was carefully laying the foundation. One by one, He chose the ancestors. They were not perfect by any means, but worthy of the position He conferred on each. He built the bridge from the first Adam, the son of God, to the Second Adam, Jesus, the Son of Mary, the Son of God.

It did not matter that polygamy, harlotry, adultery, and incest were found among Jesus's ancestors. When the time came for the Promised Seed to be born, God the Father chose a spotless vessel: Immaculate Mary, as she is called in the Catholic Church. It is a dogma of the faith, declared by Pope Pius IX on December 8, 1854. He stated that Mary was conceived free from original sin, which all of humankind has inherited from Adam and Eve. This was a special grace, unmerited favor bestowed on her by God. It is representative of Jesus's saving grace bestowed on all: Redemption by His death on the cross. A dogma is a doctrine revealed by God.

Young Mary, His handmaiden, unblemished, innocent, pure, holy, good, truthful, and full of love, was handpicked to bear God's beloved Son, who was also Handpicked, Unblemished, Innocent, Pure, Holy, Good, and full of Truth and Love. God's wisdom is Infinite.

Mary was God's best choice for bringing our Lord and Savior into this corrupt world. No man questioned the Father's choice of

---

[1] Robert Jamieson, A. R. Fausset, and David Brown, *Commentary Critical and Explanatory on the Whole Bible* (Grand Rapids, MI: Christian Classic Ethereal Library, n. d.), http://www.ccel.org/ccel/jamieson/jfb.xi.iii.iii.html, Luke 2:35.

mother to raise His Son to manhood. When she visited her cousin Elizabeth, the latter burst forth into "a magnificent canticle, in which the strain of Hannah's ancient song, in like circumstances, is caught up, and just slightly modified, and sublimed."[2] This song is commonly called the Magnificat.

When redemption's work finally had to be accomplished, how utterly wretched and vulnerable Mary was. Her entire being felt Jesus's pain and longed to comfort Him. Innumerable times in her mind, she must have replayed and relived every moment from the time Gabriel announced she was highly favored to the violent, heartbreaking scene of her beloved Jesus being nailed to the cross.

What mother would stand by and let her child suffer if she had any power at all to rescue that child? But Mary was powerless. All she could do was stand at the foot of the cross and weep. Her heart was so tormented and fragmented, the tears just flowed unimpeded. But her pain was not invisible to or unnoticed by her suffering Son. He gave John, His beloved disciple, to her as her son, and she to him as his mother: "Woman, behold your son!" In other words, He was no longer just her son, but the Son of Man, Savior of all.

Mary always knew Jesus was born for a purpose and was about His Father's business. Now, in the fulfillment of that purpose, she had to find comfort in the arms of a new son. John from that moment embraced her, which Wesley calls a peculiar honor that Jesus bestowed on John. Absolutely! John was now replacing Jesus as Mary's earthly son.

There are many times in life when we become as defenseless as Mary was then, when there seems to be no way out. But Mary was perfectly positioned, humble and unashamed at the feet of Jesus, and He reached out to His mother to comfort her. If we learn to be in the right place—at the foot of the cross, no matter how great the pain—and if we learn to be patient and humble, Jesus will always reach out to us and dry our tears. We must have the faith to just let go and let Him be God.

---

[2] Jamieson, et al., *Commentary*, Luke 1:46-55.

Mary came to that point where, as heart-wrenching as it was, she had to let go of her Son and let Him be God, all by Himself. She was expressly informed from the beginning that the Child she would bring forth was the Son of God. Joseph was told that His name would be Jesus, because He was destined to save His people from their sins. When, where, and how were not specified, but both parents were told. The Bible tells us even from Gabriel's visit to the birth of Jesus and beyond, Mary pondered these things in her heart.

Weeping endures for a night or two or three, but joy comes again. Mary did not have to wait any length of time to hear that Jesus was again alive and seen by many. He had the victory after all! *He was God.* Her Son accomplished what no human being could have done. Jesus, Son of Mary, was truly now revealed as Jesus, Son of God.

Mary, Mother of God, has become the most revered woman in the world, honored not just by Christians but by various religious sects. In August 2004, Reuters News Service reported from Lourdes, France, and the Sanctuary of Fátima in Portugal that Muslims, Hindus, Buddhists, and other pilgrims were frequenting these famous Catholic shrines to worship the Virgin Mary. Some even venerated the statues of her as they do their own goddesses.

Only one woman is named in the Koran: Mariam, the mother of Jesus. Chapter 3 is entitled "Family of Mariam," and chapter 19, "Mariam." Chapter 3, verse 34 describes Mary's immaculate nature: that she was born without original sin, never committed any sin in her life, and remained a virgin. Chapter 50, verse 23 speaks of her going to heaven in her physical body, referred to as the Assumption of Mary.

She is considered by some to have had no other children, but this is erroneous. When Jesus was teaching one Sabbath in the synagogue, and all were astounded by His knowledge, the people asked, "Is this not the carpenter, the Son of Mary, and brother of James, Joses, Judas, and Simon? And are not His sisters here with us?" (Mark 6:3).

Today, many young girls defile themselves before marriage. The sentiment is that everyone is doing it, so it is not a big deal.

But it is a big deal. If Mary had not been chaste and pure before God, she could not have obtained the honor and favor bestowed upon her. She was immaculate. Young girls should not allow what others do to dictate their own actions, nor allow peer pressure to railroad them to conform. Most of all, they should protect themselves from getting into compromising situations. There is a saying that playing with fire burns.

Unprepared for motherhood, many girls are forced to give up their babies for adoption, because there is no Joseph in their lives to do the right thing and protect them. Time and time again, young men disavow their involvement and run away, leaving girls to deal with the situation alone. I appeal to all of you, especially to young girls, to try to live holy before God. It matters to God. It should matter to you too.

The adulterous woman in the Bible was caught in the very act by her accusers, yet she alone was brought before Jesus. Adultery, which means sex with someone other than your married partner, was greatly frowned upon in the Bible. Though many take greater liberty in today's world, adultery cannot be condoned. Many marriages have been destroyed because of extramarital relations.

When Judah heard that Tamar was with child, adultery was the reason he gave for wanting to burn her to death, because she was supposedly betrothed to his youngest son, Shelah. Again, no thought was given to the male perpetrator. Had Tamar not cunningly proven her case, she alone would have been put to death. The double standard still persists. It seems little has changed over the centuries.

I know of a couple who married recently. The young woman was resolute: she was going to wait until she found the man of her dreams, and be married before she indulged in sexual relations. She met her husband-to-be about three years ago. The date for their wedding was set. As the young groom hugged his mother on his way to his wedding ceremony, he said to her, "Mom, I never did anything before." She felt very proud that that was his testimony on his wedding day.

It was a beautiful wedding. There was a special aura of innocence and purity that permeated the atmosphere. This couple had proved that even in today's world, they were able to fall in love, get engaged, and wait to be married. They are great role models for youths. Their minds were made up to do the right thing, to be in God's will. Their strength, the willpower to persevere, came from praying together. They prayed about everything. Most of their praying was done over the phone. They proved that prayer works.

Parents, remember that you play an incomparable role in the lives of your children. In fact, you have been informed by the Holy Scripture how you should bring up your child. The burden is on you to train up your children in the fear and admonition of the Lord, so that as they grow, they will not depart from what was instilled in them, but will grow in grace before God, even as Mary and Joseph did for Jesus: "and the Child grew and became strong in spirit, filled with wisdom, and the grace of God was upon Him" (Luke 2:40).

CHAPTER 16

OTHER WOMEN OF FAITH IN THE BIBLE

T he women discussed in this work do not in any way exhaust the list of all women of faith in the Bible. There is Delilah, who never gave up until she learned the source of Samson's strength, much to his detriment (Judg. 16:4–22). There is Dorcas or Tabitha, a disciple whom Peter restored to life. "This woman was full of good works and charitable deeds which she did" (Acts 9:36). And there are more, like the women I describe in more detail below.

Leah and Rachel

Leah, meaning *weary*, was Laban's elder daughter, and not as beautiful as her younger sister, Rachel. Jacob was sent to Laban, Rebekah's brother in Padan Aram, when he had to flee from Esau, his brother. He fell in love with Rachel and agreed to work seven years for her hand in marriage. On the evening of the wedding, unbeknown to Jacob, Laban gave Leah to him instead. When Jacob realized he had been hoodwinked, Laban explained that traditionally, the older sister had to be married before the younger. Jacob agreed to work another seven years for his second wife, Rachel, meaning *ewe, the daughter*. Leah had to live knowing she was unloved by her husband. Rachel remained barren for many years, jealous of her sister's fertility. Their stories can be found in Genesis 29 through 35.

Shiphrah and Puah

Shiphrah and Puah, midwives to enslaved Hebrew women, were Egyptian idol worshippers like Hagar. They were commanded by Pharaoh, "'When you do the duties of a midwife for the Hebrew women, and see *them* on the birthstools, if it *is* a son, then you shall kill him; but if it *is* a daughter, then she shall live.' But the midwives feared God, and did not do as the king of Egypt commanded them, but saved the male children alive" (Exod. 1:16–17). They showed great faith by risking their lives. God showed them favor and provided households for them. Because of their faith in and fear of God, Moses was kept alive after his birth, and grew up to be used mightily by God.

Bathsheba

Bathsheba is named the daughter of Eliam in 2 Samuel 11:3, and wife of Uriah the Hittite. In 1 Chronicles 3:5, she is daughter of Ammiel and wife of David. King David espied Bathsheba one day while she was bathing. Although he learned she was the wife of one of his soldiers, he was overcome by her beauty, sent for her, and committed adultery. She became pregnant and sent word to the king, trusting him to fix the problem. And he did. When he could not convince Uriah to go home and lie with his wife, David sent Uriah into the heat of battle, where he was likely to be killed. Uriah was. David married Bathsheba, and the son conceived in adultery died shortly after birth. She later bore Solomon, who became the heir to the throne. Bathsheba held David to his promise to allow Solomon to ascend the throne. She is part of the genealogy of Jesus Christ.

Mary Magdalene

Jesus went through cities and villages, healing and preaching the good news of the kingdom. Among His audience were "certain women who had been healed of evil spirits and infirmities—Mary called Magdalene, out of whom had come seven demons, and Joanna the wife of Chuza, Herod's steward, and Susanna, and many others who provided for Him from their substance" (Luke 8:2–3). Mary of Magdala and these other women were simply showing gratitude for their healing. They became disciples of Jesus. Mary Magdalene was there at the foot of the cross, saw where Jesus was buried, and was one of the women who, on that glorious Sunday morning, discovered that the tomb was empty. She is not to be confused with the sinner woman of Luke 7:36–50.

The Samaritan Woman

A Samaritan woman encountered Jesus at Jacob's Well as she came to draw water. He asked her for a drink. She wondered how could He ask for a drink, when Samaritans and Jews did not interact. A conversation ensued, and she desired the Living Water He offered her. Jesus told her to go and get her husband; she said she did not have a husband. Jesus told her she had spoken truthfully, because she had had five husbands, and the man she currently lived with was not one of them.

The Samaritan woman realized that Jesus was a prophet. She was so convinced that she left her water pot, went into the city, and began to evangelize: "'Come, see a Man who told me all things that I ever did. Could this be the Christ?' ... And many of the Samaritans of that city believed in Him because of the word of the woman who testified, 'He told me all that I *ever* did'" (John 4:29, 39).

Phoebe

Paul personally recommended certain women of faith, including Phoebe, who was a member of the church in Cenchrea, a harbor in Corinth. "I commend to you Phoebe our sister, who is a servant of the church in Cenchrea, that you may receive her in the Lord in a manner worthy of the saints, and assist her in whatever business she has need of you: for indeed she has been a helper of many and of myself also" (Rom. 16:1–2).

Priscilla, Aquila, and Others

"Greet Priscilla and Aquila, my fellow workers in Christ Jesus, who risked their own necks for my life, to whom not only I give thanks, but also all the churches of the Gentiles. Likewise *greet* the church that is in their house ... Greet Tryphena and Tryphosa, who have labored in the Lord. Greet the beloved Persis, who labored much in the Lord" (Rom. 16:3–5, 12).

***

These are real women who lived during Bible times, in both the Old and New Testaments. Their stories are not recounted by chance. God uses their lives as examples to help us discriminate between good and evil, right and wrong, as we struggle daily to take up our cross and follow our Savior, Jesus Christ. Today we can draw strength, wisdom, and most of all faith from their examples as we read about their lives.

The Bible is alive. The Word of God will continue to echo throughout time, as His love, compassion, and correction are encountered from generation to generation. We read the Holy Bible as His instructions for life and His way of keeping in touch with His children. May your faith increase daily.

CHAPTER 17

SAINT JOAN OF ARC (AD 1412–1431)

Visions of a Peasant Girl

Saint Joan of Arc unmistakably ranks with Deborah the judge, and Esther the queen of Persia. Warrior, militant, and martyr, she was one of those who diligently sought the Lord, and led the French army to victory under His divine guidance. The French army defeated the British in the Hundred Years' War.

Joan, born January 1412 in Domrémy, France, was a peasant, daughter of Isabelle and Jacques d'Arc, who were devoutly religious. Joan never learned to read and write, but a great love for the Catholic Church and its teachings was inculcated in her by her pious mother.

Joan knew that her life was not like those of her peers because of the personal, spiritual encounters she experienced. She was never found playing and dancing in the streets like other girls her age, nor did she swear. She was frequently in church, praying. Her first vision occurred in 1424, at age twelve, in her father's garden.

> Joan sensed she was surrounded by a great light.
> She also heard, as she said later, "a revelation

> from God by a voice," which told her to be devout, to pray, to frequent the sacraments, and always to rely on the Lord for help ... The third time this happened, Joan knew that she heard the "voice of an angel," as she put it ... Over the next three years she was summoned by the voices "to come to the aid of the king of France."[1]

According to Mary Gordon, Joan first heard voices instructing her she must "preserve her virginity for the salvation of her soul," and later, to be supportive of Charles VII, the heir to the throne, and save France.[2] She believed she heard the voices of three saints: St. Michael the Archangel, St. Margaret, and St. Catherine. Spoto states that in Hebrew thought, God's presence and actions among His people were dramatically represented by angels. "In medieval France Michael the Archangel was the special patron of soldiers fighting against faithless armies: he was always invoked with prayerful songs amid battles. The flags of the dauphin himself were painted with Michael's image."[3] In the Bible, Archangel Michael is mentioned in Jude 1:9.

Catherine of Alexandria was honored by Christians in medieval Europe, but was quietly removed from the list of Catholic saints in 1969, because the story told of the eighteen-year-old—violently tortured and imprisoned under Maximinus, eventually beheaded during the persecutions of Christians circa AD 235–238—proved to be "wildly fictitious" and was no longer considered part of the canon. Statues of her were found throughout France, and many chapels were dedicated to her in Europe.

> She was the primary patroness of young girls and of students who had to debate learned colleagues and professors; in other words, Catherine was

---

[1] Donald Spoto, *Joan: The Mysterious Life of the Heretic Who Became a Saint* (San Francisco: HarperCollins, 2007), 14.

[2] Mary Gordon, *Joan of Arc* (New York: Penguin, 2000), xx.

[3] Spoto, *Joan*, 17.

just the sort of heroine Joan herself would have taken for model and intercessor, a saint whose name and reputation had been close to her since childhood and to whom she would naturally turn during the harrowing year of her imprisonment and interrogation.[4]

Margaret of Antioch, like Catherine, supposedly lived during the persecution of the early Christians, and was specially honored in the region where Joan was born and raised. Margaret was disowned by her pagan father when she converted to Christianity and dedicated her virginity to God. When she refused a young man who tried to seduce her, "he publicly denounced her as a Christian, and after numerous tortures she too was beheaded. She became the special patroness of falsely accused people, and her statue had a prominent place in Joan's parish church. Margaret was precisely the kind of young, courageous virgin whose fidelity unto death would have comforted Joan during her interrogations."[5]

During Joan's lifetime, France was occupied by the British and their Burgundian allies. Joan believed God had chosen her to lead France to victory in the long-running war, later known as the Hundred Years' War, 1337–1453. Joan's home was situated between the two factions; many had already become refugees, leaving their houses and all their possessions behind, because of the bitter conflict.

Joan took her calling seriously. At sixteen, in May 1428, she went to Vaucouleurs to the regional governor, seeking permission to go to the dauphin in Chinon. "She insisted that it was her divinely ordered mission to take charge of the French army, defeat the English, and escort Charles to Rheims to have him properly

---

[4] Ibid., 19.

[5] Ibid., 19–20.

crowned king."[6] She was promptly dismissed. That did not deter this ambitious and courageous young girl. As the saying goes, a good "man" cannot be kept down.

Military Support and the Siege of Orléans

The following year, Joan returned and gained success. The governor provided her with a small escort to take her to the dauphin, and her two brothers joined her. When Joan arrived at Chinon and presented herself to Charles, her hair was cut short and she was dressed as a man, but she made it clear to all she was a girl.

She was given her first test. Charles disguised himself as an ordinary citizen and stood among three hundred or more of his supporters. Joan had never met him, but "if Joan was all that she was rumored to be, then her purity of heart should enable her to detect the king of France amid a vast throng. This was a standard test of spiritual discernment."[7] Joan approached him the moment she entered the hall. Later, in their private conversation, she recounted personal things that he said he had only uttered in secret to God.

By April 1429, she had persuaded Charles to provide her with a horse, a suit of armor, and weapons, and to place her at the head of the army marching to rescue Orléans. "She had her standard painted with an image of Christ in Judgment and a banner made bearing the name of Jesus. When the question of a sword was brought up, she declared that it would be found in the church of Sainte-Catherine-de-Fierbois, and one was in fact discovered there."[8]

---

[6] Stephen Richey, *Joan of Arc: A Military Appreciation* (2000), Saint Joan of Arc Center, (Albuquerque, N.M.) accessed March, 2017, http://www.stjoan-center. com/military/stephenr.html, 2nd paragraph.

[7] Spoto, *Joan*, 48.

[8] Malcolm G.A. Vale and Yvonne Lanhers, Saint Joan of Arc, *Encyclopædia Britannica, Inc.*, 2016, accessed June 26, 2017, http://www.britannica.com/ biography/Saint-Joan-of-Arc, Joan's Mission.

When Joan came on the scene in Orléans, it had been under siege since October 1428 by the British and the Burgundians, the last step before a full occupation of France. The French army had suffered years of humiliation in battle. Charles heeded her urgent plea to head the army, because every rational and orthodox option had been tried without result. In fact, Charles was at the point of conceding the battle.

The record indicates that Joan effectively turned the longstanding Anglo-French conflict into a religious war—a perilous strategy to say the least, since she could be considered a sorceress or a heretic. If Joan was deemed as such, Charles's enemies would surely use it against him. To circumvent this, the dauphin ordered background inquiries and a theological examination by Poitiers theologians in order to ascertain Joan's moral character. Poitiers is a city southwest of Paris. The commission of inquiry that was set up, including about eighteen members, concluded that she was a good, virtuous Christian, full of humility, simplicity, and honesty. This was in April 1429.

The siege of Orléans was another test. Joan had great success, and the long-drawn-out conflict with the English ended in victory for the French. She was acknowledged as the heroine, though she was wounded. The fortress was taken and the defeated English army retreated the next day.

Joan demonstrated tremendous courage and mental acumen. She adopted her own strategy at Orléans, having victories at the fortress of Saint Loup and Saint Jean le Blanc. During another siege carried out against the main stronghold of the English in Les Tourelles, on May 7, three days after her former victories, she was shot in the neck with an arrow. This did not deter her from a quick return to the battlefield.

Due to Joan's success, the French army began to support and reevaluate further aggressive moves as the war progressed.

Reims, Coronation of a King

Besides liberating France from occupation by the English, Joan had also been directed by her angel voices to ensure the coronation of the dauphin. She therefore had to get Charles and the army to Reims, the traditional place for French coronations since AD 816. Dressed in men's clothing with her hair cropped, she made her way to Reims.

> Bertrand de Poulengy: " ... I and Jean de Metz, with the help of the other people of Vaucouleurs, arranged that she give up her female clothes, which were red in color, and we had them make for her a tunic and male clothing, spurs, greaves, a sword, and the like, and also a horse; and then I, with Joan and my servant Julian, Jean de Metz' servant Jean de Honecourt, Colet de Vienne and Richard l'Archier, took to the road to go before the Dauphin."[9]

Charles was a very weak leader and a procrastinator. Joan had to encourage him to hurry to Reims for his coronation. While traveling with him, she led several detachments of troops on sorties. As they passed through extremely hostile territory, they conquered many cities. The king-elect arrived safely for his coronation. Finally, on July 17, 1429, Joan was present at Reims Cathedral when King Charles VII was crowned. That day, she knelt before him and saluted him as king for the first time.

Gordon stresses that the victory in Orléans and Charles's coronation greatly boosted Joan's power. Because she prompted popular action, she drew more and more people to her side. Charles's army grew larger than ever. Joan was to Charles what Deborah was to Barak in the Bible. Charles was not a strong

---

[9] Allen Williamson, Biography of Joan of Arc (Jeanne d'Arc), *Joan of Arc Archive*, 2000-2014, accessed March 30, 2016, http://www.joan-of-arc.org/joanofarc_life_summary_vaucouleurs.html, Segment 3: Vancouleurs.

leader, but Joan's faith and energy as the boy/girl on horseback elevated his dormant hopes. She continually assured him of his legitimacy as king. He soon realized that Joan was not a fly-by-night curiosity; she was there to stay, and he could not restrain her.

> Charles and Joan illustrate a phenomenon that occurs when young women want to move from the realm of the symbolic, where male imagination has placed them, to the realm of the actual, where they want to be. A girl can be an ornament, but if she wants to act rather than be looked at, if she wants scope and autonomy rather than the static faith of the regarded, even the well-regarded, object, she becomes dangerous. Joan had not changed; she was, rather, misread.[10]

Injury and Failure

Joan was restless and disillusioned by the apathy demonstrated by the king, and soon implored him to mount an offensive against Paris, another stronghold of the British. Charles was hoping that Phillip of Burgundy would simply surrender Paris to him. When this failed, he provided some troops to Joan and her team to launch an assault on September 8. Joan was wounded in the leg by a crossbow, but she would not relent. That night, some of her men finally removed her against her will.

So great was her determination, strength, and zeal to lead her people to victory, she was back on the battlefield the next morning. She kept fighting but was given a royal order to desist, withdraw, and meet the king at Saint-Denis. He made the army abandon the attack on Paris.

Charles insisted she attend court, but Joan felt out of place and utterly useless there. He was conducting secret negotiations with Burgundy and was encouraged to get Joan out of the way by sending her to battle. He provided her with some troops, and

---

[10] Gordon, *Joan*, 66–7.

she had one victory over the English at Saint-Pierre-le-Moûtier, southeast of Bourges. But her resources were insufficient for the next assault on La Charité. She begged for assistance from neighboring towns and the nobility, but no help arrived. She eventually abandoned the mission.

Captured

In the spring of 1430, she undertook a mission for King Charles VII, against a Burgundian assault on Compiégne. On her way, Joan tried to capture a Burgundian post at Margny, but the enemy forces numbered six thousand men, and she and her meager army failed. Joan took another route. On May 23, her army took Margny. But the Burgundians had beefed up their army by that time, and the French found themselves significantly outnumbered. They hastened to retreat to Compiégne. Joan was with the rear guard, her usual position, as the army withdrew.

The captain of the town, seeing the huge number of Burgundian soldiers about to cross into his town, raised the drawbridge. Joan and a few of her men were shut out; she was caught and pulled from her horse as the Burgundian troops surrounded the rear guard.

She agreed to surrender to a pro-Burgundian nobleman. "From that moment, late in the afternoon of Tuesday, May 23, 1430, Joan was a prisoner, and so she remained for the rest of her life."[11] The Burgundians brought her to the English commander in Rouen, exchanging her for ten thousand livres. Little did she know that the wheels of a great conspiracy were fast turning to try her for heresy. Ultimately, they would exact her life as punishment.

Imprisonment and Trial

Joan was cast into prison with no one to turn to but God. "In the trial that followed, Joan was ordered to answer to some 70

---

[11] Spoto, *Joan*, 112.

charges against her, including witchcraft, heresy and dressing like a man. The Anglo-Burgundians were aiming to get rid of the young leader as well as discredit Charles, who owed his coronation to her. In attempting to distance himself from an accused heretic and witch, the French king made no attempt to negotiate Joan's release."[12]

The Word of God says do not put your trust in man or in chariots and horses. No good deed goes unpunished. As much as Joan of Arc had done for France, and risked her life through enemy territory to make sure Charles VII was crowned king, and though he had knowledge from the learned theologians at Poitiers that she was neither heretic nor witch, Charles failed to lend Joan his support.

He knew that the lifting of the siege of Orléans had been her biggest test. She had not only been successful, but had earned the respect of many, including prominent clergymen such as the Archbishop of Embrun and Jean Gerson, a theologian. These men enthusiastically endorsed Joan by writing treatises immediately after her victory in Orléans. There was more than enough proof of the innocence of this young Christian warrior to save her from the outrageous charges made.

Joan was charged as a heretic, apostate, idolater, sorceress, and cross-dresser. The trial was politically motivated and extremely biased, breaking all legal ethics. The opposition was determined to establish guilt by any means possible. They were unscrupulous and without mercy—so very afraid of an uneducated teenage girl, in whom the power of God was undoubtedly at work. There were no grounds for a trial because the clerical notary found nothing criminal in Joan's behavior. Yet Bishop Cauchon, an English supporter, got the court to begin a trial with members of the tribunal, all of them pro-English clergy.

At the opening of the trial, Joan asked for clergy who were pro-French to be included in the tribunal, in order to establish some measure of balance. She was flatly denied. She was also

[12] History.com Staff, Joan of Arc: From Witch to Saint, *History.com*, 2009, accessed June 7, 2015, http://www.history.com/topics/saint-joan-of-arc.

disallowed counsel. Both of these denials were violations of church law. But this travesty of justice was allowed to continue.

Coley Taylor notes, in his introduction to a translation of her trial by W. P. Barrett, there has surely been no more horrible or dramatic trial in history than hers. Joan was the only witness called in her defense.

> We see Jeanne pitted against sixty skilled politicians, lawyers, ambassadors, trained in all the complexities of legal questioning, all of them versed in academic casuistry. Most of them were avowedly her enemies. Her victories for Charles VII had driven many of them, including Bishop Cauchon, out of their dioceses, away from their seats of authority and revenue. They were of the University of Paris and Jeanne had threatened Paris. If she had succeeded in that they would have been utterly ruined.[13]

> The world had seen nothing like her since Christ. The judges and assessors at Rouen knew as they assembled there that the eyes of Christendom were upon them and that dynasties trembled in the balance. They also were aware that the King of Heaven spoke through His saints. They knew that Jeanne had prophesied that she would raise the siege of Orléans and had done so. They knew that she had prophesied she would have the Dauphin crowned at Reims.[14]

Under the threat of death, after being imprisoned for one year, Joan was forced to sign a confession recanting her claim to any

---

[13] Paul Halsall, *Medieval Sourcebook: The Trial of Joan of Arc*, Fordham University, 1999, accessed March 31, 2016, http://sourcebooks.fordham.edu/halsall/basis/joanofarc-trial.asp, x. [Original Source: W. P. Barrett, *The Trial of Jeanne D' Arc*, trans. Coley Taylor and Ruth H. Kerr, (Gotham House, Inc., 1932), x].

[14] Ibid., xi.

divine guidance whatever. Several days later, she was condemned to death by the powers that be because she had dared to put on men's attire. This was considered heresy and a capital crime because it was a repeat offense. She had repeated the offense because Cauchon had forced her guards to threaten her with rape and take away her dress. She was left no choice but to wear the men's clothes the guards threw at her. "Several eyewitnesses remembered that Cauchon came out of the prison and exclaimed to the Earl of Warwick and other English commanders waiting outside: 'Farewell, be of good cheer, it is done!', implying that he had orchestrated the trap that the guards had set for her."[15]

Lo, I Am With You

Joan, the Maid of Orléans, was burned at the stake on May 30, 1431, even as she forgave her accusers.

> They tied her to a tall pillar well above the crowd. She asked for a cross, which one sympathetic English soldier tried to provide by making a small one out of wood. A crucifix was brought from the nearby church and Friar Martin Ladvenu held it up in front of her until the flames rose. Several eyewitnesses recalled that she repeatedly screamed "... in a loud voice the holy name of Jesus, and implored and invoked without ceasing the aid of the saints of Paradise". Then her head drooped, and it was over.[16]

Joan received strength to suffer such a grotesque death by looking at a crucifix, the symbol of the crucifixion of Jesus Christ, while she prayed.

---

[15] Allen Williamson, Biography of Joan of Arc (Jeanne d'Arc), *Joan of Arc Archive*, 2000-2014, accessed March 31, 2016, http://archive.joan-of-arc.org/joanofarc_short_biography.html#trial, The Trial.

[16] Ibid.

Jean Tressard, Secretary to the King of England, was seen returning from the execution exclaiming in great agitation, "We are all ruined, for a good and holy person was burned." The Cardinal of England himself and the Bishop of Therouanne, brother of the same John of Luxembourg whose troops had captured Joan, were said to have wept bitterly. The executioner, Geoffroy Therage, confessed to Martin Ladvenu and Isambart de la Pierre afterwards, saying that "... he had a great fear of being damned, [as] he had burned a saint." The worried English authorities tried to put a stop to any further talk of this sort by punishing those few who were willing to publicly speak out in her favor: the legal records show a number of prosecutions during the following days.[17]

When the centurion and those who were guarding Jesus witnessed the earthquake and all the signs and wonders that manifested as He yielded His Spirit, they too had to confess that truly He was the Son of God.

Stephen, the first martyr of the church, was stoned to death because of his confession of faith in the Lord Jesus Christ. He also found strength to go through:

[A]nd they cast *him* out of the city and stoned *him*. And the witnesses laid down their clothes at the feet of a young man named Saul. And they stoned Stephen as he was calling on *God* and saying, "Lord Jesus, receive my spirit." Then he knelt down and cried out with a loud voice, "Lord, do not charge them with this sin." And when he had said this, he fell asleep. (Acts 7:58–60)

As Stephen was stoned, a young man, full of zeal, witnessed

---

[17] Ibid.

his death. His name was Saul, a persecutor of Christians. But soon enough, the Lord confronted him and he surrendered. Saul became Paul, and Jesus said to Ananias, "For I will show him how many things he [Paul] must suffer for My name's sake" (Acts 9:16). Paul experienced many things, and through them all, he learned that God's grace was sufficient for him.

Christ Himself had to suffer the infamous death on the cross. He asked His Father, if it was possible, that the cup be removed from Him. But He was quick to acknowledge, "Nevertheless not My will but Your will be done." He was strengthened in the garden of Gethsemane when angels came and ministered to Him. Even nailed to the cross, He cried out, "Father forgive them for they know not what they do."

It was this example that Stephen and Joan were able to follow, and plead that no guilt be ascribed to their accusers. All of Jesus's apostles except John, the beloved, experienced suffering and violent deaths for His name's sake. They endured to the end.

Young Joan of Arc, the Maid of Orléans, knew who was the source of her strength. As she did in life, so Joan did in her ordeal of death, looking unto her Lord and Savior Jesus Christ, from whence all her help had come, who gave her the victory in battle though she was a young, inexperienced peasant girl without a formal education. God gave her wisdom beyond her years; undeniably, He used the foolish things of the earth to confound the wise.

"Asked if she knows she is in God's grace, she answered: 'If I am not, may God put me there; and if I am, may God so keep me. I should be the saddest creature in the world if I knew I were not in His grace.'"[18] This question was a religious trap by the scholarly: an affirmative answer would result in a heresy charge, and a negative answer meant confessing her guilt. The interrogators were dumbfounded by the adeptness of her response. That's why Jesus says not to worry what you will answer them: "Now when they bring you to the synagogues and magistrates and authorities, take no thought, do not worry about how or what you should answer, or what you should say. For the Holy Spirit will teach you in that very hour what you ought to say" (Luke 12:11–12).

Joan's virginity was one of the paramount things she cherished. She had the wisdom to know she was in a man's world and had to protect herself, which was what led to the charge of cross-dressing. She wore male attire and cut her hair so she would not be recognized as a female and taken advantage of by unscrupulous males. Her haircut was the inspiration for the popular bob hairstyle in the twentieth century. In his introduction to Bernard Shaw's *Saint Joan*, Joley Wood makes mention of this: "Joan's battle savvy and instincts were that of a soldier, so it was perfectly logical to her to be dressing and acting as such. This is a person achieving her potential, not a destiny determined by gender – and how would a 'womanly' woman be treated in a camp of soldiers? Not as a soldier. Joan did the commonsensical thing and was persecuted for it."[18] [19]

Imprisoned, Joan continued to wear men's attire to protect herself from rape. During her trial, she reported that a great English lord had come to the prison and tried to rape her when she was wearing female attire. As a teenage girl, she did what she thought best to avoid unsolicited advances by treacherous members of the opposite sex.

Not much has changed over the centuries in this department. Rape and incest are at epidemic proportions in society. David had to deal with it when his son Amnon raped his half sister Tamar. Absalom, her brother, sought revenge by killing Amnon.

Today many young girls and women are at risk of being raped, even in their homes, not only by strangers but by very close family members and friends. Individual, gang, statutory, and other types of rape are well documented in today's world. Young boys are also targeted.

From the scandalous accounts of high-profile Hollywood celebrities to the unheard stories of the very poor in the slums

---

[18] Paul Halsall, *Medieval Sourcebook: The Trial of Joan of Arc,* Fordham University, 1999, accessed March 31, 2016, http://sourcebooks.fordham.edu/halsall/basis/joanofarc-trial.asp, 52. [Original Source: W. P. Barrett, *The Trial of Jeanne D' Arc,* trans. Coley Taylor and Ruth H. Kerr, (Gotham House, Inc., 1932), 52].

[19] Joley Wood, introduction to *Saint Joan,* by Bernard Shaw (London: Penguin, 1923), xx.

of India, the drum echoes with a resounding beat from city to city, country to country, century to century, and is barely heard by the masses who are so busy with life, as in the days of Noah. This news is routinely in the media. As modern as this twenty-first-century society claims to be, no remedy has been found to deter such repulsive and dehumanizing conduct. Even when the architects of these heinous crimes are released from prison as sex offenders, with mandatory reporting of their whereabouts, some still manage to strike again.

Joan knew she had no other means but wearing male attire to ward off the dangerous, unsolicited advances of the sex offenders of her day.

Retrial and Canonization

Much has been said and written about Joan of Arc. Original records have been recovered concerning her life and, especially, her trial. Joan became even more famous following her execution. She achieved mythical stature many years before she was beatified in 1909, and ultimately canonized by Pope Benedict XV in 1920.

Her mother, Isabelle, did not forget her child, and fought to clear her daughter's name. Her formal statement to the court reads:

> I had a daughter born in lawful wedlock, who grew up amid the fields and pastures. I had her baptized and confirmed and brought her up in the fear of God. I taught her respect for the traditions of the Church, and I succeeded so well that she spent most of her time in church, and after going to confession, she received the Eucharist frequently. Because the people suffered so much, she had a great compassion for them in her heart, and despite her youth she would fast and pray for them with great devotion and fervor. She never thought, spoke or did anything against the faith. But certain enemies had her arraigned

in a religious trial. Despite her disclaimers and appeals, both tacit and expressed, and without any help given to her defense, she was put through a perfidious, violent, iniquitous and sinful trial. The judges condemned her falsely, damnably and criminally and put her to death in a cruel manner by fire. I demand that her name be restored.[20]

Twenty-four years after the Hundred Years' War ended, a posthumous retrial opened. Sanctioned by Pope Callixtus III, this "rehabilitation trial," also known as the "nullification trial," was initiated at the request of the inquisitor-general, Jean Bréhal, and Joan's mother, Isabelle Romée. A total of 115 witnesses testified. Bishop Cauchon, who had passed away, was convicted posthumously of heresy for convicting Joan, an innocent woman, purely out of revenge.

Joan of Arc was declared a martyr. On July 7, 1456, she was deemed innocent and cleared of all charges. Cross-dressing was rightly allowed for the purpose of self-preservation, or to hide oneself from the enemy, according to the guidelines stated by St. Thomas Aquinas.[21]

Viewpoint

At age twelve, Joan heard the voices of angels describing her life's mission of saving her country. Reminiscent of Moses and his excuses when God commissioned him at the burning bush to go and deliver His people Israel, Joan too had excuses. Spoto tells us she at first protested that she was just a poor girl and was unable to ride a warhorse or lead men in battle. Very soon she could no longer ignore the voices, "and she placed her

---

[20] Spoto, *Joan*, 197–8.

[21] Allen Wiilliamson, Joan of Arc: Theological Points Concerning the Male Clothing Issue, *Joan of Arc Archive*, 2002- 2003, accessed March 31, 2016, http://www.archive.joan-of-arc.org/joanofarc_male_clothing_theology.html.

honor and her faith in God, Who, she was assured, would supply what she lacked."[22] The Bible states, "But seek first the kingdom of God and His righteousness, and all these things shall be added to you" (Matt. 6:33).

All the time she was imprisoned, Joan never heard from Charles. He never once reached out to her. She fell out of favor and was punished because she was too headstrong, too independent. Despite the lack of support from Charles, "what is remarkable is that she never seemed to resent this; she died believing him worthy of her love and her devotion, the anointed of the Lord, anointed with the sacred oil of Clovis that shone on his temples because of her."[23] Like King David, she knew to respect the anointed of God. The success he achieved twenty-five years after her martyrdom could not have been accomplished without the groundwork she laid.

Joan was burned at the stake for wearing garments that were supposedly only for men. Imagine what the members of that tribunal would do or say if they beheld the women of today! Six centuries later, female cross-dressing has become the norm. Most women today would feel disenfranchised if told they could no longer wear pants.

Thankfully, today we are under the dispensation of grace and not the Law. God looks at the heart, not the clothing. He tells us in the book of Joel that we should rend our hearts and not our garments. Joan's heart was in the right place, full of love for her heavenly King, Jesus Christ, and for her earthly king and country.

In the words of Spoto:

> Neither wife nor nun, neither queen nor noblewoman, neither philosopher nor stateswoman, Joan of Arc represents something that was fresh then and is still pertinent now for anyone, and perhaps most poignantly for women. In the final analysis, her battle was not with English politicians

---

[22] Spoto, *Joan*, 14.

[23] Gordon, *Joan*, 71.

but with the powerful of the Church. Dedicated to her faith, she was betrayed by its earthly institution; abandoned by everyone for whom she fought, she was blithely handed over to a death that was illegally maneuvered and hideously exacted. In her terror, her loneliness, and her agony she remains a figure of starkest simplicity.[24]

Joan was not actively involved in combat while she was commander of the French army, but like Deborah, she accompanied her soldiers into battle as a source of inspiration. She plotted strategic, military, and diplomatic moves against the enemy. She took no weapon into battle but held her banner high. For the short period she was their commander in chief, the French army experienced outstanding victories.

At the tender age of nineteen, Joan, her name meaning *gift from God*, or *God is gracious*, had singlehandedly transformed French military tactics by her aggressive use of frontal assaults and artillery. The methods she introduced were employed for the remainder of the war, which lasted twenty-four years after her execution. The gratitude she received was death by burning at the stake. She drew strength from her Maker, with whom she had had a personal relationship for seven years. Her place among great women of faith cannot be denied. It was bought with a price that few could pay.

The Voice of A Christian

God willed: I was. What He had
planned I wrought,
That done, He called,
and now I dwell with Him.[25]

---

[24] Spoto, *Joan*, xviii.

[25] Hymnist unknown. Quoted in Stanford E. Murrell, *A Foundation for Faith: An Introductory Study of Systematic Theology with References to the Baptist Confession of Faith of 1689* (1998), (Port Richey, FL: NTS Library, n. d.), http://www.ntslibrary.com/PDF%20Books/An%20Introductory%20Study%20 of%20Systematic%20Theology.pdf, 224.

CHAPTER 18

MOTHER TERESA
(AD 1910–1997)

A Father's Death and a Calling

Agnes Gonxha (Anjezë Gonxhe) Bojaxhiu was the third and last child born to Albanian Catholic parents Nikola and Dranafile Bojaxhiu. Agnes means *rosebud* or *little flower*. She was born in the prominently Muslim city of Skopje in the Balkans (now in Macedonia). Her father was a successful businessman, and her mother stayed at home to care for the children.

Nikola died unexpectedly when Agnes was about eight. It was total devastation for the family. Dranafile found herself a single parent, having to provide for her children. Jennifer Rosenberg states that both before and especially after her husband's death, Dranafile made sure the family held tightly to their religious beliefs. Prayer was a daily ritual and they went on annual pilgrimages to the shrine of the Black Madonna of Vitina-Letnice. It was here in August 1928 that young Agnes's commitment strengthened to follow a religious life.

It is said that the family that prays together stays together. But something special was destined to take place in this family. One member would depart and make her way to a far country, and end up as one of the iconic figures of the twentieth century. Agnes, like Saint Joan of Arc and Saint Thérèse of Lisieux, felt God's call from a very early age. At age twelve, Agnes felt the calling to be a nun. This was not a simple decision. She would have to give up all hope of what we call a normal life—having a family of her own—and leave her biological family behind.

Heeding the Call

We must learn to discern when God is speaking to us. Hannah's son Samuel, as a young lad with Eli the priest, had to learn to respond to God's call upon his life. Agnes was no different. For five years she heard the call of God and thought about becoming a nun. She continued helping her mother organize church events, feed and care for the poor, and sing in the church choir. Then the time came for that final decision.

When God called Abraham, He commanded him, "Get out of your country and from your relatives, and come to a land that I will show you" (Acts 7:3). Agnes was compelled to leave her native land and embark upon a course that would eventually lead her to the land she was destined to inherit.

> When Mother Teresa [Agnes] was 17, she made the difficult decision to become a nun. Having read many articles about the work Catholic missionaries were doing in India, Mother Teresa was determined to go there. Thus, Mother Teresa applied to the Loreto order of nuns, based in Ireland but with missions in India. In September 1928, 18-year-old Mother Teresa [Agnes] said goodbye to her family to travel to Ireland and then on to India. She never saw her mother or sister again.[1]

---

[1] Jennifer Rosenberg, "A Biography About Mother Teresa, the Saint of the Gutters" *ThoughtCo*, Mother Teresa updated April 6, 2017, accessed June 2, 2015, http://www.thoughtco.com/mother-teresa-1779852.

Agnes adopted the name Sister Teresa, after Saint Thérèse of Lisieux. It took more than two years for Agnes to become a Loreto nun. In Ireland, she learned the history of the Loreto Order and studied English for six weeks. On January 6, 1929, she arrived in India at the Loreto Entally Convent in Kolkata. There she began teaching geography and history at the convent schools.

Going outside the walls of the convent was not permitted to the nuns of the Loreto Order. Somehow, Mother Teresa received special authorization in 1935 to teach at St. Teresa's Convent, located outside her own convent. She was then twenty-five years old.

Two years later, Agnes Gonxha Bojaxhiu took her final vows and officially became Mother Teresa on May 24, 1937. Immediately after that, she became principal of St. Mary's Convent School, and for nine years was mandated to live within the convent.

A Call within a Call

On September 10, 1946, Mother Teresa was on a journey to Darjeeling. As she was sitting on the train, an inspiration suddenly germinated—to exit the safety of the convent and live among the poverty-stricken masses of India, rendering them assistance. This event she described as a "call within a call."

She made repeated requests to her superiors for two years, but they felt it was too dangerous for her to embark upon such a mission, and refused to give their consent. Finally, she was given one year "to help the poorest of the poor." Mother Teresa made very simple preparations before she set out upon this life-changing mission. She purchased three cheap saris made of white cotton, the edge of each lined with three blue stripes. This symbol of humility became the dress code for the nuns of the Missionaries of Charity.

On August 16, 1948, after twenty years as a nun in the Loreto Order, Mother Teresa left the safety of the convent and stepped out into the vast, dangerous world in the slums of India, just as she had left her home and family so many years ago, never to look back. This move was a giant step of faith.

The Mission

How did Agnes develop this great love for the poor and destitute? Her mother, Dranafile, was exceptional. As difficult as the family's financial situation was after her husband's death, she made sure she inculcated in her children the love and joy of sharing. It is reported that Agnes was cautioned to never eat a single mouthful of food without sharing it with others. Her mother led by example, always reaching out to the very poor by inviting them to eat with the family. Thus love for the poor was a vital part of Mother Teresa's early experience.

When she stepped out of the convent, she remained for a while in Patna, learning the basics about medicine. In December 1948, thirty-eight-year-old Mother Teresa began her lifelong missionary work in the slums of Kolkata, India. Without resources to depend on, she walked around for a bit, gathered some small children, and began to teach. She had no classroom, no desk, no chalkboard, no paper, no help—but nothing deterred her. She found a stick and began drawing letters on the ground. Officially, school was in session.

At that stage of her life, she knew she could do all things through Christ Who gave her strength. "Go, and lo I will be with you always" was Jesus's command to His apostles. She had learned to heed that directive.

Pretty soon, Mother Teresa found a hut she could rent and turned it into a classroom. In place of parent-teacher conferences, she visited the homes of the children she taught, as well as others in the area, and encouraged them with medical assistance and advice when she could. Poverty was pronounced everywhere she went. Genuine gratitude was shown for any assistance she offered. One night she took about three pounds of rice to a family. The mother took it, divided the rice in two, and hurried out the door. Later she explained that there was another family she knew who also had nothing to eat.

The first year was very tough; Mother Teresa had no money and no resources. Many times, she felt like giving up and returning to the sanctuary of the convent. She never allowed that impulse to take root.

Soon enough, word of her mission began to spread, and those of a generous nature began donating to her cause. Her very first helper, one of her previous students, came aboard in March 1949. Before she knew it, nine more former students willingly joined the mission. When God truly calls, He empowers and provides. At the end of her first year, Mother Teresa applied to form her own order of nuns. She was granted permission by Pope Pius XII. She began the Missionaries of Charity on October 7, 1950. There was much work to be done.

India ranked among the poorest countries of the world then. Mother Teresa realized millions needed help. She could only do so much; her assets were limited. The hospitals, though overflowing, took those who had a chance to survive. Others were left on the streets to die.

Mother Teresa initiated a process to rectify this problem. She received a building from the city of Kolkata, and opened the doors of the Place of the Immaculate Heart, Nirmal Hriday. Volunteer nuns went from street to street, searching out the dying. The nuns brought them in, bathed and fed them, and gave them a bed, thereby offering them a place to expire with some measure of dignity and spirituality.

The order's first orphanage was opened in 1955, called Shishu Bhavan. When it was possible a child could be adopted, arrangements were made. The other children were educated, taught a trade, and allowed to marry at the appropriate time.

Many people were infected with leprosy. Mother Teresa fought to take control of this situation too. She began a leprosy fund and initiated Leprosy Day in order to educate the populace about the disease. In addition, she created a number of mobile clinics that provided medicine and bandages for the lepers. She

154

established Shanti Nagar, the first leper colony in India, where those infected were able to independently live and work.

The Word of God says you do not light a candle and place it under a bushel. You must let your light shine before men that others may see and glorify the Father in heaven. By their tenth anniversary, the light of the Missionaries of Charity was so brightly shining, they were authorized to branch into greater territory outside of Kolkata. The cities of Ranchi, Delhi, and Jhansi opened houses, and more followed very soon. By the order's fifteenth anniversary, their work was so well-known that they were permitted to expand internationally. In 1965, the first mission was established in Venezuela. Other houses around the world followed.

Mother Teresa and her order of nuns became known nationally and internationally for their humanitarian work, and more and more houses were added to the Missionaries of Charity organization. She and her work were acknowledged worldwide. She received several awards, including India's highest civilian award, the Jewel of India. In 1979, Mother Teresa was nominated for the prestigious Nobel Peace Prize, the symbol of ultimate honor and distinctive achievement in the entire world. Mother Teresa won the Nobel that year. Her work in the slums of India was noticed, not only as a great act of humanity, but also as a means of eradicating poverty, one of the root causes of war.

In his paper "War and Poverty", Kieran Oberman argues, "Poverty can render a war unnecessary (thus violating last resort) because poverty alleviation sometimes offers an alternative means to pursue the same cause that supposedly justifies the war."[2] He concludes, "When the just cause for a war, described in morally salient terms, is something that can be achieved by means of poverty alleviation, the war is unnecessary and should not be waged."[3]

---

[2] Kieran Oberman, "War and Poverty," 2015, *Academia.edu*, accessed March 20, 2017, http://www.academia.edu/2328679/War_and_Poverty, 2.

[3] Ibid. 25-26.

Lifetime Achievements into Eternity

Her achievements were numerous, but in the end, Mother Teresa was as humble as in the beginning. Her love for the poor, the sick, the dying, and the orphaned gave her the determination and the strength to answer God's call. She left the comfort and safety of her native land behind, venturing into a far country—not to live a prodigal life, but to dedicate herself to the betterment of others who had no hope or recourse.

Mother Teresa was sure of one thing: she knew God was able to meet every need, big or small. She remained humble, but as she became known internationally, criticism increased about her methods and intentions. Her vocal approval of positions of the Catholic Church on doctrines such as opposing contraception and abortion was criticized. She said in her 1979 Nobel lecture, "I feel the greatest destroyer of peace today is abortion." She voted no to ending the Irish constitutional ban on divorce and remarriage.

The worst criticism was penned by Christopher Hitchens in his book *The Missionary Position: Mother Teresa in Theory and Practice*, in which he accused her of glorifying poverty for selfish reasons, and lending justification for the continuance of beliefs and institutions that maintain persistent poverty.

She was undaunted. Jesus Christ faced criticism from His very own people, but that did not deter Him from fulfilling His mission on earth. Mother Teresa pressed on to the mark of her high calling, the calling she had perceived when she was only twelve years old. God had brought her a mighty long way. Controversy would not intimidate her from accomplishing what God had commissioned her to do, nor did controversy hinder her from speaking out on issues of the day.

Her health deteriorated during the 1990s, but despite many illnesses, Mother Teresa refused to slow down. She continued to travel and spread her message. Finally, at age eighty-seven, on September 5, 1997, her heart gave out. She was laid to rest in Kolkata at the mother house of the Missionaries of Charity, the order of sisters she founded in 1950.

Agnes Gonxha Bojaxhiu had made up her mind at a very

early age to answer God's call and go where He led her to her life's work. She left quite a legacy: four thousand Missionary of Charity sisters in 610 centers in 123 countries. Among other honors, she was recognized with a well-earned Nobel Peace Prize, the greatest achievement in modern society. Countless lives were touched by her benevolence. She certainly can be designated, not only as a mighty woman of faith, but one of the greatest humanitarians of the twentieth century.

Even in death, it was not yet over for Mother Teresa. On October 19, 2003, she was beatified, the first step to declaring her a saint. This spiritual promotion was bestowed by Pope John Paul II, and she became Blessed Teresa of Kolkata. The consensus for beatification was prompted by the testimony of an Indian woman, Monica Besra, who attributed the miraculous healing of a tumor in her abdomen to intercession made through Mother Teresa.

More recently, a second miracle experienced by a Brazilian man was reported. Marcilio Andrino was suffering from a viral brain tumor and in a coma. His family and friends claimed that they prayed and asked for intercession through Mother Teresa. To their surprise, while he was in the operating room being prepared for emergency surgery, Marcilio awoke from his coma. He was without pain and fully cured of the tumor.

This prompted Pope Francis, on December 17, 2015, to move to declare sainthood for Blessed Teresa. On September 4, 2016, she received the highest tribute of the Catholic Church, canonization, and will forever be called Saint Teresa of Kolkata.

Viewpoint

Jesus said the poor we will have with us always. When we look around us today, we see how startlingly true this is. Those who are able to live in affluence are few, as compared to the vast number who eke out a living on a daily basis. For many, a good job is hard to come by, even after going through the process of educating themselves.

A tremendous number of men and women work at

minimum-wage jobs, which make it very difficult to provide adequately for their families. These people are numbered among the working poor. They must depend on government assistance, if available, to meet their basic needs—food, clothing, shelter. God said He will provide for all our needs. Some people are so bitter over the state of their affairs, they forget to look to the hills, to God who is the Giver of all blessings.

Full provision was made for Adam and Eve before they were placed in Eden. All the wealth of the earth belongs to God. Mother Teresa knew this when she was commissioned by God to go out into the slums of India. She had no job that brought any income, but she had faith that He who owns everything would provide for the work she had to accomplish. The great legacy she has left behind proves that God did not fail her. God cannot fail.

There is still much work to be done for the poor we will always have. We do not have to be Mother Teresa and go to a foreign land to work among them. The poor are all around us, and some of us *are* the poor. Each one of us should make it a point to share with and care for the very destitute, even as young Agnes was taught by her mother. That poor Indian family was able to share a little rice with another family, though they needed it themselves.

If you believe you cannot afford to share your physical possessions, there is always love to give. Mother Teresa gave her love, all of it, and her life. She made able disciples who are carrying on her legacy.

At her canonization, Pope Francis declared:

> Mother Teresa, in all aspects of her life, was a generous dispenser of divine mercy, making herself available for everyone through her welcome and defense of human life, those unborn and those abandoned and discarded ... For Mother Teresa, mercy was the "salt" which gave flavor to her work, it was the "light" which

shone in the darkness of the many who no longer
had tears to shed for their poverty and suffering.[4]

King Solomon left us the book of Proverbs, and his father, King
David, was the author of many of the Psalms. Mother Teresa left
us numerous quotations, proverbs of her own that, if employed,
can foster excellent and valuable life lessons for many in ministry,
and to the layman. Jone Johnson Lewis, a women's history expert,
has put together a select list of these quotations, some of which
are included below:

1. Love is doing small things with great love.
2. I believe in love and compassion.
3. Do not wait for leaders. Do it alone, person to person.
4. Kind words can be short and easy to speak, but their echoes are truly endless.
5. Suffering is a great gift of God.
6. We think sometimes that poverty is only being hungry, naked and homeless. The poverty of being unwanted, unloved and uncared for is the greatest poverty. We must start in our own homes to remedy this kind of poverty.
7. The dying, the cripple, the mental, the unwanted, the unloved—they are Jesus in disguise.
8. It is not how much we do, but how much love we put in the doing. It is not how much we give, but how much love we put in the giving.
9. I do not pray for success. I ask for faithfulness.
10. God does not call us to be successful. He calls us to be faithful.[5]

---

[4] Pope Francis, "Homily" from Holy Mass and Canonization of Blessed Mother Teresa of Calcutta, *Saint Peter's Square*, September 4, 2016, accessed Feb. 16, 2017, http://w2.vatican.va/content/francesco/en/homilies/2016/documents/papa-francesco_20160904_omelia-canonizzazione-madre-teresa.html.

[5] Jone Johnson Lewis, "Mother Teresa Quotes. Saint Teresa of Calcutta (1910–1997)" *ThoughtCo*, updated June 14, 2017, https://www.thoughtco.com/mother-teresa-1779852, The Most Memorable Mother Teresa Quotes.

Jesus, in speaking of those who will inherit the kingdom of heaven because of their righteous works of feeding, clothing, sheltering, and visiting the sick and the imprisoned, states, "Assuredly, I say to you, inasmuch as you did *it* to one of the least of these My brethren, you did *it* to Me" (Matt. 25:40). All must be done as unto Him.

Jesus is our example. He went around doing good all the time, and Mother Teresa learned to do the same. As she says, we should not be satisfied by just giving money; we need to give our hearts, to give love everywhere we go. Love is giving, and we are nothing without it. We say God is love; He gave His Son to us. The great love that our Creator demonstrates is referenced in the most famous passage of Holy Scripture: "God so loved the world that He gave His only begotten Son that whosoever believeth in Him shall not perish but have everlasting life. (John 3:16).

Mother Teresa manifested this selfless, agape love her entire life. She gave and gave of herself until her heart gave out. In fact, she lived by the fruit of the Spirit: joy, peace, love, goodness, kindness, gentleness, faithfulness, long suffering, and self-control. You shall know them by their fruits. This wonderful woman of God lived for others, bearing good fruit. Her life can be summed up in her very own words: "It is not how much we do, but how much love we put in the doing. It is not how much we give, but how much love we put in the giving."

When we find it difficult to reach out to others, remember Mother Teresa, who took her cue from the Son of God, Jesus Christ. He gave all His love and laid down His life on Calvary, so you and I can have life and have it more abundantly. That is why He came. That is why He made a binding covenant with His Father—to redeem us from sin and hell, no matter what it took, and teach us the way to heaven, reversing the effects of what Eve brought into the world by her great act of disobedience.

Even as Eve finally learned to trust God, her Maker, no less is required of us. Trust Him for all things. Trust Him knowing that He promised He will never leave us or forsake us. Jesus asked, "Nevertheless, when the Son of Man comes, will He really find faith on the earth?" (Luke 18:8). Will men still believe He is God and trust Him unconditionally? Mother Teresa kept the faith, ran her race, finished her course, and obtained her crown of glory, sainthood.

CHAPTER 19

OPRAH WINFREY (1954–)

Rise to Fame

Oprah Winfrey, included on the *Forbes* List 2016, is categorized as one of the most powerful women in the world. She is best known for her nationally syndicated talk show, *The Oprah Winfrey Show*, which aired from 1986 to 2011. It was the highest-ranked show of its kind, quickly surpassing *The Phil Donahue Show*, the number-one-rated show when Oprah first came on the air.

Born into poverty of a single mother in Mississippi, Oprah always had faith that she would become somebody. The little girl who was so poor that she wore dresses made from potato sacks, who endured teasing and criticism from her peers because of her poverty, who was sexually molested during her young life, today is noted as the twentieth century's most affluent and only known African American billionaire, per *Forbes* magazine. She is known internationally as a media giant, television host, producer, entrepreneur, actress, and great philanthropist. She was recognized by *Life* magazine as the most powerful woman of her generation. She launched the *Oprah Winfrey Network* (OWN) in January 2011, and it is now owned by *Harpo Productions* and *Discovery Communications*.

Humble Beginnings

The woman we know as Oprah was born Orpah Gail Winfrey on January 29, 1954. Either the midwife or the record clerk transposed the "rp" to "pr" in her first name, and "Oprah" was written on her birth certificate.

Oprah was brought up by her grandparents in their three-bedroom farmhouse, with very little access to her mother. Hattie Mae, her grandmother, took full control of her upbringing until she was six.

> "Momma," as she called her grandmother, was strict but loving. She instilled in Oprah reverence for God and the habit of daily prayer. "Momma" also taught Bible stories to Oprah. The Faith United Mississippi Baptist Church played an important role in Oprah's early years. . .At the age of three, she gave her first public speech at church, "Jesus Rose on Easter Sunday." Adults were always impressed with the precocious little girl.[1]

Church meant attending Sunday school, then morning service from eleven to two thirty. Dinner was eaten on the front church grounds, then it was back into church for service at four. Oprah was well-known for reciting verses from the Bible: "Oprah because of her grandmother knew how to read, and write before the age of three. Oprah during church would recite poems, and verses from the bible. Soon the church, and the entire neighborhood knew she had a gift and was nicknamed, 'The Little Speaker'."[2] She must have recited, "I can do all things through Christ who strengthens me" (Phil. 4:13).

---

[1] Judith Janda Presnall, *Oprah Winfrey* (San Diego, CA: Lucent Books, 1999), 14.

[2] Peter Sean, "Oprah Winfrey Biography," *IMDb.com*, 1990-2017, http://www.imdb.com/name/nm0001856/bio?ref_=nm_ov_bio_sm.

As a young person, she was very vocal in assuring everyone she was going to be somebody. She was going to be very rich.

Instability and Rape

At age six, Oprah moved to Milwaukee with her mother, Vernita Lee, who by that time had another daughter, and a boyfriend who promised marriage and a house. They all lived in one room in a noisy, dirty neighborhood. Her mother worked long hours as a maid, leaving early and returning late, but she loved having her girls with her.

When Oprah was eight, due to financial reasons, she was sent to live with her father and stepmother, Vernon and Zelma Winfrey. This was in 1962. It was a challenging and stimulating environment for the eight-year-old. Zelma taught her multiplication tables that summer to prepare her for third grade. She was required to learn a certain number of vocabulary words, read one book, and write a book report each week.

Oprah shone both socially and academically, impressing all with her verbal abilities. Church and Sunday school continued to be an integral part of her life. Then she went to her mother for the summer vacation, and when Vernon came to get her for the new school year, Vernita refused to let her go, much to Oprah's dismay.

Vernita wanted her family together. She had a new man and another child. This time, home was a two-bedroom apartment in Milwaukee. But there was not any parental supervision. Unfortunately, at age nine, Oprah was raped by a nineteen-year-old cousin. Later on, a trusted family friend and an uncle did the same to her.

Scarred but Defiant

Oprah was afraid to speak to anyone about being molested because she felt she would be blamed. She lived a very tortured young life—she blamed herself, and her self-esteem eroded.

Through it all, Oprah had one thing none could take from

her—God had blessed her with supreme intellect. She was a naturally gifted student. This was not overlooked by one of her teachers, Eugene A. Abrams. He helped her obtain a scholarship to a wealthy private school in the Foxpoint suburb.

The experience of a new school in a rich neighborhood, and of observing how the other side lived, made her poverty seem even more austere. She began telling lies about her background, stole money from her mother, hung out with the wrong crowd, and became sexually active, hoping to receive love and attention. Her sexual promiscuity resulted from her earlier encounters with rape, which were many. Her delinquent behavior escalated until, at fourteen, she became pregnant.

Vernita knew she could no longer take care of or control her daughter. In desperation, she again called Vernon Winfrey. He drove to Milwaukee to take his daughter back to Nashville. He was appalled and saddened by Oprah's pregnancy and all that he heard about her. The baby was born prematurely and died two weeks later. Oprah realized she had been given a second chance. God always gives chances.

Father Knows Best

Thank God for wisdom. Vernon was very strict and oversaw every aspect of Oprah's life, from what she wore to her language. It was time for tough love. No heavy makeup—if she disobeyed, he sat her down and took it off before she left the house. He was to be called "Daddy," not "Pops." "Vernon would not tolerate any questioning of his rules. He had a favorite saying: "Listen, girl—if I tell you a mosquito can pull a wagon, don't ask me no questions. Just hitch him up!'"[3]

He did not accept Cs on her report card, letting her know that because he knew she was capable of better, Cs were not permitted in his house. Now, as a high schooler, Oprah was required to read five books every two weeks, write reports on them, and learn five new words each day. She was introduced to some African

---

[3] Presnall, *Oprah*, 24.

American authors. She enjoyed reading about women who had gone through tough times. She credits Maya Angelou's *I Know Why the Caged Bird Sings* as instrumental in helping her overcome the abusive experiences encountered in Milwaukee.

Oprah became an extremely accomplished student, was voted the most popular girl in her class at age sixteen, which did not impress Vernon one bit. He felt "Most Likely to Succeed" was a more important title. She ran for and became school president.

Church was never neglected. It was the centerpiece of her life, the solid foundation that Hattie Mae had built from the cradle. Oprah had several speaking engagements in churches as far afield as Los Angeles. On that trip to Hollywood, she visited the Hollywood Walk of Fame and told her father she would definitely have a star there one day—so great was her faith, self-assurance, and drive to succeed.

She entered various beauty contests, and her personality, confidence, talent, and speaking skills always worked for her. "I had marvelous poise and talent and could handle any questions, and I would always win in the talent part, which was usually a dramatic reading. I could—I still can—hold my own easily. Ask me anything, and my policy has always been to be honest, to tell the truth. Don't try to think of something to say. Just say whatever is the truth."[4]

In one contest, the three finalists were asked what would they do if they were given a million dollars. The other two girls said they would spend it on the poor and on family. Oprah said if she were given a million dollars, she would be a spending *fool*! Her brash, humorous answer made her the winner of that beauty contest.

Oprah credits her father for profoundly transforming her life, and says he is the one to whom she owes her great success. "When my father took me, it change the course of my life … He saved me. He simply knew what he wanted and expected. He would take nothing less."[5] "And you, fathers, do not provoke

---

[4] Ibid., 30–1.

[5] Ibid., 27.

your children to wrath, but bring them up in the training and admonition of the Lord" (Eph. 6:4). Vernon Winfrey did. Thanks be to God!

All Grown Up

When Oprah moved to Baltimore to work, she began speaking at city schools and mentoring young girls. In third grade, she heard Jesse Jackson speak, and something he said lit a fire in her and changed her view of life. He said excellence was the best deterrent to racism; excellence was the best deterrent to sexism. She always read a great deal. Reading, she insists, is the strongest signal for future success. This brings to mind President Barack Obama, an avid reader, whose mother woke him very early to teach him English when he lived in Indonesia. We have all seen the fruits of her labor.

Oprah attended Bethel AME in Baltimore. Every week, she was at Sunday service, always sitting in the same seat at the center of the second row. She became well-known and beloved in the African American community by supporting local politicians and through her many speaking engagements. It was also in Baltimore she met her lifelong friend, Gayle King, a production assistant. They both worked at the same news station.

Oprah's biographers reveal a great deal about her life and all its ups and downs on her way to the top. Kitty Kelly in particular lays it all bare. But Jesus accepts us as we are. Throughout Oprah's life, she has remained connected to God, the source of her strength. Once, when a vicious false rumor was spread about her, what kept her was a Bible verse: "'No weapon that is formed against thee shall prosper; and every tongue that shall rise against thee in judgment thou shalt condemn' And this I know, no matter how difficult things may get, this I know."[6]

Remembering the trauma she suffered because of that rumor, Oprah noted, "I have been hurt and disappointed by things that

---

[6] Kitty Kelly, *Oprah: A Biography*, (New York, Crown Publishing Group, a division of Random House, Inc., 2010), 207.

people have said and tried to do to me, but through it all, even in my moments of great pain ... I had the blessed assurance that I am God's child ... And nobody else's. That is really the source of my strength, my power. It is the source of all my success."[7]

Oprah continues to mentor teenagers, hoping to steer them in the right direction. A few of her famous quotations are:

> Be thankful for what you have; you'll end up having more. If you concentrate on what you don't have, you will never, ever have enough.

> What kind of woman do I want to be? One who willingly gives and receives love. One who is compassionate. Understanding. Positive. Forgiving. A woman who makes responsible choices. I want to live with a heart open to life.

> Doing the best at this moment puts you in the best place for the next moment.

> The more positive you are about life, the more positive it will be. The more you complain, the more miserable you will be.

> The whole point of being alive is to evolve into the complete person you were intended to be.

In a commencement speech in 2009 at Duke University in Durham, North Carolina, she said to her success is being able to be of service to others. She received America's highest civilian award, the Presidential Medal of Freedom, from President Barack Obama in 2013. In 2002, she became the first recipient of the Academy of Television Arts & Sciences' Bob Hope Humanitarian Award.

---

[7] Ibid. 207. Oprah Winfrey, "Personal Quotes (29)," *IMDb.com*, 1990-2017, http://www.imdb.com/name/nm0001856/bio?ref =nm_ov_bio_sm.

Besides being a humanitarian, Ms. Winfrey is an activist dedicated to children's rights, and has been for a very long time. She made a proposition to Congress to initiate a bill for a national database of convicted child molesters; it was signed into law in 1994 by President Bill Clinton. This was a major piece of legislation in answer to the stifled cries of the children of abuse.

Viewpoint

Oprah has shown love, and is beloved by millions the world over whose only encounter with her has been on their television screens. They have forged a bond with the little girl who dared to be somebody; who was so sure she would succeed, so sure she would be great someday. She strove for excellence and reached the highest pinnacles. She earned her star on the Hollywood Walk of Fame in 2010, just as she said she would.

Whether she was on top of the mountain or way down in the valley, through the good and the bad, she was always able to pick up the pieces and keep going, because she knew she was never alone. She learned that way back in Faith United Mississippi Baptist Church, before she could talk, read, or write. She could say in the words of the hymn writer:

> I've seen the lightning flashing, and heard the thunder roll,
> I've felt sin's breakers dashing, trying to conquer my soul;
> I've heard the voice of my Savior, telling me still to fight on,
> He promised never to leave me, never to leave me alone.

> Refrain:
> No, never alone, No, never alone;
> He promised never to leave me,
> Never to leave me alone.

The world's fierce winds are blowing, temptation's sharp and keen,
I have a peace in knowing my Savior stands between—
He stands to shield me from danger, when earthly friends are gone,
He promised never to leave me, never to leave me alone.

When in affliction's valley I'm treading the road of care,
My Savior helps me to carry my cross when heavy to bear,
Though all around me is darkness, earthly joys all flown;
My Savior whispers His promise, "I never will leave thee alone."

He died for me on the mountain, for me they pierced His side,
For me He opened the fountain, the crimson, cleansing tide;
For me He's waiting in glory, seated upon His throne,
He promised never to leave me, never to leave me alone.[8]

She is a woman of faith. We will never know the innumerable lives she has impacted and still does, the many she has given hope, and helped to reach within, to dig deep and find the faith to capture and pursue their dreams. May God continue to bless her as she fulfills His purpose for her life.

She still prays on her knees and reads the Bible daily. As Hattie

---

[8] Anonymous, "Never Alone," 1892.

Mae told her, "As long as you have the power to bow your head and bend your knees, you do it and God will hear you better."[9]

> Train up a child in the way he should go,
> And when he is old he will not depart from it.
> (Prov. 22:6)

Lessons well taught. Lessons well learned.

---

[9] Presnall, *Oprah*, 14.

CHAPTER 20

MALALA YOUSAFZAI
(1997–)

Firstborn

Malala Yousafzai, a young activist and humanitarian, was born July 12, 1997, in Mingora, Pakistan, to parents Ziauddin and Toor Pekai Yousafzai. When she was born, her father added her name to the family tree, which was an unusual thing to do. Only male children's names were typically added to the family tree in Pakistan, but Ziauddin made no distinction between her and her two younger brothers, Khushal and Atal.

Malala is a Pashtun, a proud tribe of people found in Afghanistan and Pakistan. She was nicknamed Jani by her father, Persian for *dear one*, and Pisho by her mother, which means *kitten* in Pashto.

Early Childhood

Malala attended the Khushal School for Girls, founded by her father three years before she was born. Besides being a school owner, he is an education and anti-Taliban activist and poet. The family lived in Swat Valley. There was not much money left for food after salaries and rent, but Ziauddin still provided free education to one hundred children.

Unlike in Afghanistan, girls in Pakistan were free to attend school, but many of Malala's cousins and friends in the village did not go to school. Mostly, girls were not considered important, especially by their fathers, who thought it a waste of time and resources to educate daughters who would marry young and move to their husbands' homes.

Luckily for Malala, her father made sure she attend school daily. He often discussed politics with her after her brothers were in bed. He knew his daughter was special and treated her so. Her father has been one of the primary educators in her life. Malala is fluent in Urdu, Pashto, and English.

Growing up, she saw adult women cover their faces when in public. She told her parents she would not cover her face when she was grown. Relatives objected, but her father stated that she could do whatever she wanted. She was beloved by her father. He told everyone Malala would live as free as a bird. She had heard from her father what the Taliban in Afghanistan was doing to women, who were compelled to wear a severe head-to-toe veil called a *burqa*. Schools for girls had been burned down.

A Letter to God

One day Malala went to throw garbage out on the heap because her brothers were not available to do that chore. To her dismay, she discovered a girl her age, full of sores, sorting garbage into piles. Other young boys were searching for bits of metal. She was too scared to talk to them, but when her father came home, she took him to see them. With tears in his eyes, he told her they were working to sell whatever they could get from the garbage to feed their families. They did not go to school.

Malala decided to bring the problem to God:

> *Dear God*, I wrote in a letter. *Did you know there are children who are forced to work in the rubbish*

heap? I stopped. Of course he knew! Then I realized that it was his will that *I* had seen them. He was showing me what my life might be like if I couldn't go to school. . .Now I knew *I* would have to do something. I didn't know what it was. But I asked God for *the strength and courage to make the world a better place.*[1]

She saw her mother with an extra pot of rice and chicken, and inquired why she always gave food away. Toor Pekai responded they knew what it was like to be hungry; thus they always shared what they had. They shared everything, including their home with a family of seven who were experiencing hard times. Like Agnes, Malala was learning what it means to love one another and be your brother's keeper.

Drastic Change

In 2005, a devastating earthquake measuring 7.6 on the Richter scale rocked the Swat Valley. Tehrik-e-Nifaz-e-Sharia-e-Mohammadi (TNSM) was the first to offer assistance. This was a branch of the Movement for the Enforcement of Islamic Law, a militant group. Maulana Fazlullah was one of the leaders.

Very soon Radio Mullah began condemning anything Western as un-Islamic and sinful, instilling fear in the people. The voice on the radio turned out to be that of Maulana Fazlullah, a high school dropout without any religious qualifications. He said God would send another earthquake if they did not conform to sharia, a form of Islamic law that required all aspects of life to be overseen by religious judges.

A reign of terror escalated as Fazlullah joined forces with the Taliban. Without warning, Swat was in the throes of a terrorist war. There were suicide bombings, curfews, deaths by flogging, and beheadings. Life was becoming a total hell. Malala's father refused

[1] Malala Yousafzai, *I Am Malala*, with Patricia McCormick (New York: Little Brown, 2014), 26–7.

to close his chain of schools known as the Khushal Public School, despite the fact that students kept dropping out, especially the girls.

Regardless of the threats and the burning down of other schools, Ziauddin began to speak out against the Taliban. A threatening note was left on his school gate by the Taliban, but Ziauddin was not going to disenfranchise the girls and boys who, in spite of the danger, made their way to school.

Malala was very bright and loved school. One night she answered the door and a mufti (an Islamic scholar) and some elders entered. Her father sent her inside, but she heard their conversation. The mufti said he was a representative of good Muslims, "and we all think your girls' high school is a blasphemy. You should close it. Teenage girls should not be going to school. They should be in *purdah*."[2] This meant girls should hide themselves at home, keeping out of sight of men and strangers.

Media Exposure

Malala practiced making speeches in front of her mirror, thinking that one day she would be speaking to the world. In 2008, her father and Madam Maryam, their teacher, worked with the girls to prepare essays and speeches to express their feelings against the Taliban. To their surprise, a TV crew from Pashto came to the assembly. Malala says some of the girls were nervous, but she had been interviewed before. When it was her turn, she did not hesitate.

> "This is not the Stone Age," I said. "But it feels like we are going backward. Girls are getting more deprived of our rights." I spoke about how much I loved school. About how important it was to keep learning. "We are afraid of no one, and we will continue our education. This is our dream." And I knew in that instant that it wasn't me, Malala,

---

[2] Ibid., 32.

speaking; my voice was the voice of so many others who wanted to speak but couldn't.[3]

At age ten, this was her first public speech. She addressed the Taliban for imposing their values and denying her and other girls an education. As young as she was, she was a fearless advocate for their rights. The Word of God avows,

> Out of the mouth of babes and nursing infants You have ordained strength, Because of Your enemies, That You may silence the enemy and the avenger. (Ps. 8:2)

As the attacks on Swat continued in 2008, Malala spoke out on radio, in the newspapers, and on the national TV stations to anyone who would listen. The Taliban sent out a message: "After the fifteenth of January, no girl, whether big or little, shall go to school. Otherwise, you know what we can do. And the parents and the school principal will be responsible."[4] Many girls stayed home. Malala always had a prayer. She prayed to God for the courage to fight to extend the number of school days, and to appreciate those that were left.

Gul Makai

Just then, the *British Broadcasting Corporation* (BBC) contacted Malala's father, looking for someone, either a teacher or a student, to write a diary for its Urdu website about life under the Taliban. When her father could get no one else, Malala volunteered. "Why not me?" Both her parents agreed. Initially, she received help from a BBC correspondent to write the diary. He suggested, for her safety, that she not use her name.

Under the pseudonym Gul Makai (cornflower), Malala, now eleven, began blogging for the BBC in 2009, courageously

---

[3] Ibid., 71.

[4] Ibid., 73.

speaking out about life in the Swat Valley under the Taliban. She could not tell anyone, especially at school, that she was the anonymous Pakistani schoolgirl they were all raving about. Her identity was accidentally unmasked by her father, and after that her days with the BBC were numbered. But life in Swat, under the Taliban, had reached the world, including the *New York Times*.

Fazlullah and his men got their way, and all girls' schools closed. Malala and Ziauddin continued their crusade, attending events and rallies, spreading their message. Malala took advantage of every opportunity to do interviews regarding the right of girls to an education.

False Peace

Eventually, the government made a peace treaty to impose sharia if the Taliban agreed to stop fighting. The biggest TV station, GEO TV, interviewed Malala concerning her response to the peace deal. After the interview, her father's friend was stunned to learn she was only eleven, so wise beyond her years.

But the Taliban did not keep their side of the deal. They became emboldened, and violence doubled. It was time for the Yousafzai family to seek shelter elsewhere, along with two million others who were fleeing their homes. They were now labeled IDPs—internally displaced persons.

After three months, they returned to Swat and found their home pretty much intact. The boys' pet chickens had died, but Malala found her precious books exactly where she had hidden them. The Khushal School had been occupied by the army and needed repairs. School would open again, but in secret, under Madam Maryam. Malala was overjoyed.

In early 2011, the Taliban again began blowing up schools and murdering people. In May 2011, Osama bin Laden was killed in Abbottabad, a town through which the family had recently passed. Malala's father received another anonymous death threat by letter.

Just and Unjust Rewards

Malala was used to winning awards. She had won more than forty golden plastic cups and trophies for being the top student in her class. She also won some award money for her Swat campaign for peace and advocacy for girls' education. Her voice was being heard far beyond the borders of Pakistan.

In October 2011, she was nominated by Archbishop Desmond Tutu from South Africa, for the international peace prize of Kids Rights. A week later she was awarded Pakistani's first National Peace Prize, thereafter awarded annually as the Malala Prize. She did not know then that her life was in danger. Rather, she always feared for her father, who had received death threats, because he was so avidly vocal against the Taliban. She was aware that some of his friends had already been killed by the terrorists.

The threats to the family escalated. Instead of walking the five minutes to school with her books hidden under her scarf, her mother insisted she take the bus with other girls. Early in 2012, a death threat from the Taliban came specifically for Malala. She and her father were at GEO TV when it was drawn to his attention. When he accessed her name on the Internet, the message said, *Malala Yousafzai must be killed.*

Her father was visibly shaken. He wanted them to take a break from campaigning. Malala reminded him that he was the one who had said that if you believe in something greater than your life, then even if you are dead, your voice will only multiply. Now was not the time to stop.

Later, she mused on what her reaction would be if a Talib came to kill her.

Her silent answer was that of a true feminist: just let him know her heart's desire was for education for herself, for all girls, for his daughter, for his sister, and for him.

Yet She Lives

On Tuesday, October 9, 2012, Malala was scheduled to take

her Pakistani studies exam, and studied until late Monday night. She rushed out on Tuesday morning, took her exam, and felt good about it. Her aim, as always, was to top the class. Then, "on her way home from school, a man boarded the bus Malala was riding in and demanded to know which girl was Malala. When her friends looked toward Malala, her location was given away. The gunman fired at her, hitting Malala in the left side of her head."[5] She was the only one with her face uncovered. Malala says she never heard him ask who she was, nor did she hear the *crack, crack, crack* of the three bullets. The last thing she remembered was thinking of her next exam. Malala and her friends Kainat and Shazia were shot.

The enemy could not silence her. Many may call it luck, but it was a miracle—God's divine protection manifested in Malala's life. The bus driver immediately made his way to the hospital in Mingora. Although the bullet had penetrated the left side of her head and traveled down her neck, the doctors declared Malala had not suffered any major brain damage.

Soon the army took her to Peshawar to the combined military hospital, where Colonel Junaid, a neurosurgeon, discovered that the doctors in Swat had been incorrect. The bullet had traveled very close to her brain. He obtained permission from her parents to remove part of her skull because her brain was swelling and needed room to expand. Time was of the essence.

That surgery saved her life. The piece of skull was placed under the skin of her abdomen. But two days later, her condition worsened.

Leave Your Homeland

As God willed, Dr. Fiona Reynolds and Dr. Javid Kayani, two British doctors, were in Pakistan assisting army doctors. They mandated her removal to another army hospital in Rawalpindi. If Malala did not receive advanced treatment, then brain damage

---

[5] Biography.com Editors, "Malala Yousafzai Biography.com": Targeted by the Taliban," *The Biography.com website* (A&E Television Networks, last updated April 13, 2017), accessed March 31, 2016, http://www.biography.com/people/malala-yousafzai-21362253#initial-activism.

or, even worse, death would occur. The final decision to move her to Queen Elizabeth Hospital in Birmingham, England, was made by Dr. Fiona.

Malala's father made the choice to stay behind and protect the rest of the family. It was not an easy decision. He told Dr. Javid, "What has happened to my daughter has happened ... Now she is in God's hands. I must stay with the rest of my family ... Isn't it a miracle you all happened to be here when Malala was shot?"[6] Dr. Javid responded that he believed God sent the solution first and the problem after. They induced a coma in Malala and transported her to England on a United Arab Emirates private jet, fully equipped with a medical unit. Coma or not, she was leaving her country.

Malala finally awoke on October 16, 2012, in Birmingham, with a tube in her throat.

Her first thought was to thank God that she was not dead. She had no idea that the entire world had heard about what had happened, and many were praying for her recovery. She received cards from children, politicians, journalists, and celebrities, along with teddy bears and boxes of chocolate. She was blown away by all the love she received. When she was finally able to watch the *BBC News*, she realized she *was* the news.

Together Again

Malala longed for her beloved family. They arrived on October 25, 2012. Little by little they filled in the missing pieces of her memory. She learned Shazia had been hit in the left collarbone and palm, and Kainat's arm had been grazed by one of the bullets. Both girls were recovering. The only one arrested for the attack was the poor bus driver.

The Taliban had taken responsibility, declaring Malala's campaign for girls' education and peace was obscene. Since she continued to speak out against them, they were "forced" to shoot her. Malala's response was a verse her mother had quoted to her from the Quran: "Truth will always triumph over falsehood. This

---

[6] Yousafzai, *I Am Malala*, 160–1.

is the true Islamic belief that has guided us on our journey. The Taliban shot me to try to silence me. Instead, the whole world was listening to my message now."[7]

How ironic. "And we know that all things work together for good to those who love God, to those who are the called according to *His* purpose" (Rom. 8:28). God definitely was at work in Malala's life. As she said in her book, people prayed to God to spare her, and she was spared for a reason – to use her life for helping people.

Her memory was slowly returning; she was learning to walk, talk, and read again. Her road to recovery was still a long, hard one, but she was resilient. The facial nerve that allowed her to smile, open and shut her left eye, and raise her left eyebrow had been severed by the bullet. Surgery to repair it took almost eight hours. The doctors operated behind her ear, and found that her eardrum had been shattered.

Three more major surgeries were scheduled in one day: a titanium plate was put in her head, the piece of skull was removed from her abdomen, and a cochlear implant was placed deep in her ear, with a receiver outside. She could hear again! Five days after these surgeries, she was in the family's new home in Birmingham.

On March 19, 2013, she began school in Birmingham, at Edgbaston High School, wearing a British schoolgirl's uniform instead of her familiar *shalwar* and *kamiz*, the long, loose pants and blouse she used to wear at the Khushal School for Girls.

She had not forgotten the friends she left behind. She stayed in touch through Skype. She learned she scored 100 percent on her Pakistani studies test taken that fatal day.

Higher Heights, Deeper Depths

Malala's life has changed radically. In addition to keeping up her grades, she has been very busy making speeches, documentaries, and books, while doing social media campaigns and humanitarian work. She meets exciting people and travels a great deal. Malala is

---

[7] Ibid., 164.

now a high-profile international personality, fulfilling the vision that has been so dear to her for more than half her twenty years.

On her sixteenth birthday, July 12, 2013, the first ever Youth Takeover of the United Nations was facilitated by the president of the UN General Assembly, UN special envoy for global education, former British prime minister Gordon Brown, the organization *A World at School*, and other partners. Hundreds of young advocates for education from around the world were brought in. Malala addressed the UN Assembly, her first public speech since the attempt on her life by the Taliban:

> In the name of God, The Most Beneficent, The Most Merciful.
>
> Honourable UN Secretary General Mr. Ban Ki-moon ... but first of all thank you to God for whom we all are equal and thank you to every person who has prayed for my fast recovery and new life. I cannot believe how much love people have shown me ... I speak not for myself, but so those without a voice can be heard ... My dreams are the same ... One child, one teacher, one pen, and one book can change the world. Education is the only solution. Education First.[8]

As she heard the thundering applause, she thought, by the grace of God, that she was really addressing millions of people. UN Secretary-General Ban Ki-moon described her as "a brave and gentle advocate of peace who through the simple act of going to school became a global teacher."[9]

---

[8] Malala Yousafzai UN Speech, the full text, *The Independent*, July 12, 2013, accessed March 31, 2016. http://www.independent.co.uk/news/world/asia/the-full-text-malala-yousafzai-delivers-defiant-riposte-to-taliban-militants-with-speech-to-the-un-8706606.html.

[9] Biography.com Editors, "Malala Yousafzai Biography.com": After the Attack, The Biography.com website, (A&E Television Networks, last updated April 13, 2017).accessed March 31, 2016, http://www.biography.com/people/malala-yousafzai-21362253#after-the-attack.

Seeking to Change Lives

This young activist of peace is not trying to put a Band-Aid on the problem. She is seeking real change, addressing the source of the problem from the very root. Malala believes that terrorism can only be quenched through education, and governments need to change their policies to ensure that all children get a quality education. Children should be taught the values of harmony and friendship in society, and tolerance, patience and love for each other.[10]

Malala has been quoted as saying:

> I am only talking about education, women's rights and peace. I want poverty to end in tomorrow's Pakistan. I want every girl in Pakistan to go to school.

> Education is neither eastern nor western. Education is education and it's the right of every human being.[10]

> If I win Nobel Peace Prize, it would be a great opportunity for me, but if I don't get it, it's not important because my goal is not to get Nobel Peace Prize, my goal is to get peace and my goal is to see the education of every child.[11]

> Our men think earning money and ordering around others is where power lies. They don't think power is in the hands of the woman who takes care of everyone all day long, and gives birth to their children.

---

[10] Rhiannon Mills, "Malala: Education Key in Fight Against Terror" *Sky News*, March 31, 2016, accessed March 31, 2016, https://uk.news.yahoo.com/malala-education-key-fight-against-terror-155105923.html.

I raise up my voice-not so I can shout but so that those without a voice can be heard...we cannot succeed when half of us are held back.

We human beings don't realize how great God is. He has given us an extraordinary brain and a sensitive loving heart. He has blessed us with two lips to talk and express our feelings, two eyes which see a world of colours and beauty, two feet which walk on the road of life, two hands to work for us, and two ears to hear the words of love. As I found with my ear, no one knows how much power they have in their each and every organ until they lose one.[11]

In accepting an invitation to the White House in October 2013, Malala was assured she could speak freely to President Barack Obama. He listened attentively as she chided him about drone strikes in countries like Pakistan; instead, she said, his focus should be on eradicating terrorism through education.

The Beat Goes On

Malala Yousafzai is the recipient of many prestigious awards. On October 10, 2013, in acknowledgment of her work, she was awarded the Sakharov Prize for Freedom of Thought from the European Parliament. In October 2014, she became the youngest recipient ever of the Nobel Peace Prize, an honor she shared with child activist Kailash Satyarthi. Like Mother Teresa, she was awarded the Jewel of India as well as the Nobel. In 2013, 2014, and 2015, *Time* magazine listed her as one of the most influential people in the world. She is a trailblazer, making her mark as a

---

[11] Malala Yousafzai, "Malala Yousafzai > Quotes", *Goodreads*. 2007, accessed March 21, 2016, https://www.goodreads.com/author/quotes/7064545.Malala_Yousafzai.

modern-day history maker. Blessed are the peacemakers, for more than ever today, the world needs peace.

While she was still in the hospital, numerous donations, calls, and offers to help kept pouring in. When asked what she wanted to do, she said she was fine; they should help the other Malalas. With the help of several benefactors, Malala and her father, Ziauddin, cofounded the Malala Fund.

The Malala Fund

When the Lord calls, He empowers. The first grant the Malala Fund made was used to provide schooling for forty girls, ages five to twelve, back in her village in Swat. The girls no longer had to work as domestics. Malala vowed to make the forty girls into forty million girls around the globe. She donated her Nobel Prize money, over half a million dollars, to the Malala Fund to build a secondary school for Pakistani girls.

Malala continues to raise awareness about the plight of children deprived of education in areas engulfed in conflict. The Malala Fund is financing projects, among others, in Nigeria, Kenya, Sierra Leone, Pakistan, and Jordan, where she cried over Syrian refugees.

In 2015, on her eighteenth birthday, she opened a school in Lebanon for fourteen- to eighteen-year-old Syrian refugee girls. She declared that, on her first day as an adult, on behalf of the children in the world, she was demanding that world leaders invest in books instead of bullets. She reasoned that if the world stopped spending on the military for just eight days and donated the money saved to education, the $39 billion needed to provide every child on the planet with twelve years of free, quality education would be achieved.

Viewpoint

Though so young when she began, Malala was used as a vessel of peace. Jesus still loves the little children. Malala's faith in her mission did not waver when she experienced the wrath of the Taliban firsthand. Even from her hospital bed she continued to speak out. Ironically, the assassination attempt was the cause of the first Right to Education Bill ratified by the Pakistani Parliament.

She wants to see especially girls and women treated fairly and respectfully. "The wise saying, 'The pen is mightier than the sword.' It is true. The extremists are afraid of books and pens. The power of education frightens them. They are afraid of women. The power of the voice of women frightens them."[13] An excerpt from a speech given by Michelle Obama, while still First Lady of the United States of America, states,

> "I had the pleasure of spending hours talking to some of the most amazing young women you will ever meet, young girls here in the U.S. and all around the world. And we talked about their hopes and their dreams. We talked about their aspirations. See, because many of these girls have faced unthinkable obstacles just to attend school, jeopardizing their personal safety, their freedom, risking the rejection of their families and communities.
>
> "So I thought it would be important to remind these young women how valuable and precious they are. I wanted them to understand that the measure of any society is how it treats its women and girls. And I told them that they deserve to be treated with dignity and respect, and I told them that they should disregard anyone who demeans or devalues them, and that they should make their voices heard in the world."[12]

---

[12] Michelle Obama, "First Lady Michelle Obama's Speech in Manchester, New Hampshire October 13, 2016," Glen Brown, October 14, 2016, *Blogspot. com*, (2011), accessed June 26, 2017, https://teacherpoetmusicianglenbrown. blogspot.com/2016/10/first-lady-michelle-obamas-speech-in.html

Her speech embodies and endorses Malala's sentiments, hope, and mission for girls and women. As the late James Brown said, it's a man's world, but it is nothing without women and girls.

Abraham had to get out of his country and go to a strange land. God made him the father of many nations. Moses had to leave Egypt and tend his father-in-law's sheep in Midian before God called him to leadership at the burning bush, to return to Egypt and deliver His people from slavery. God used an assassin's bullet to send Malala from her country to another, so He could better use her for His glory. "Get out of your country." He does it His way, every time.

Jesus left His home in Heaven and became the Son of Man to redeem the world from the darkness of evil. There has been no teacher greater than Him. He went around educating the masses, spreading His gospel message of peace and love to all men. He reached out to the sick, the dying, the poor, the rich, the blind, the deaf, the lame, the widow, the sinner, the Jew, and the Gentile. His message still resounds today.

As Malala said, God saved her to use her life to help others. He is using her to spread His message of peace and love. She is a voice crying in the contemporary wilderness of this sometimes selfish, loveless world for the rights of many whose voices would never be heard otherwise.

In Oslo she said, "Dear brothers and sisters, great people, who brought change, like Martin Luther King and Nelson Mandela, Mother Teresa and Aung San Suu Kyi, they once stood here on this stage. I hope the steps that Kailash Satyarthi and I have taken so far and will take on this journey will also bring change—lasting change." She is the youngest Nobel laureate and has become a symbol of peaceful protest, proving that one voice, one person, one who dares to believe can use that faith to foster change. Her inner conviction has propelled her to be a global advocate for girls' education and peace.

Malala Yousafzai may never have read the Bible or confessed Jesus Christ or been a Christian, but her philosophy and hope for all children reflect the fruit of the Spirit, even as they did for Mother Teresa. "But the fruit of the Spirit is love, joy, peace, longsuffering, kindness, goodness, faithfulness, gentleness, self-control. Against such there is no law" (Gal. 5:22–23). These are the values she has cited for children everywhere.

When Paul was called by God, he was neither apostle nor Christian. Perhaps, one day, Malala will come to know Jesus Christ as Lord and Savior of her life, and He will use her boldness, zeal, and faith, as well as the great pulpit she commands on the world stage, to draw more men, women, boys, and girls to Him. Nothing is impossible with God.

Malala wants to be a politician and, someday, the prime minister of Pakistan. Our prayers are with her. We congratulate her and thank her for all she has already accomplished. God will continue to use her for His glory.

CHAPTER 21

THEN AND NOW

From the very beginning, women have been leaving their mark, so to speak. As quiet and submissive as they have been taught to be, through the centuries women have spoken very loudly. Lives, societies, countries, and the world have all been impacted by women. Created by God for the role of wife and motherhood, women also play a vital part in the fulfillment of His plan for mankind. They are carefully chosen by Him to fulfill His mission.

Eve was not a second-class citizen. She was Adam's helpmate, his companion, his refuge from loneliness, his ishshah who was bone of his bone, magnificent to behold. Both she and Adam suffered the consequences of their breach of God's covenant. They lost the ease and abundance of Eden forever. But Eve still had all the attributes of womanhood God had bestowed upon her. She learned to trust God, even as she brought forth seed in pain. The pain of childbirth is excruciating, but is part of the legacy inherited after the fall.

There are some who choose not to have children, but for the most part, women want children. This is good for it is stated,

> Behold, children *are* a heritage from the Lord,
> The fruit of the womb *is* a reward.
> Like arrows in the hand of a warrior,

189

So *are* the children of one's youth.
Happy *is* the man who has his quiver full of them;
They shall not be ashamed,
But shall speak with their enemies in the gate.
(Ps. 127:3–5)

In the Bible, the barren woman suffered shame and reproach because she was childless. She was taunted, as Hannah was by Peninnah. The emphasis placed on the accomplishment of motherhood has driven women to great lengths. Tamar played the harlot when she felt cheated of having a child. Isaac prayed for God to open Rebekah's womb. Sarah had to wait on God and finally, at ninety, was blessed with Isaac. Hannah vowed to dedicate her son to God's service.

In contemporary times, several avenues are available for women who face such challenges: fertility treatment options, total bed rest throughout pregnancy, and surgical stitching of the uterus to avoid miscarriage, among others. Some use a surrogate or adopt or, when all else fails, steal, as Ann Pettway did. Whatever the means, women seek children, for we see children as one of the defining factors of womanhood. It is God's way of replenishing the human race. After the Flood, He told Noah and his sons, "Be fruitful and multiply, and fill the earth" (Gen. 9:1). That could not have been realized without their wives, the four women handpicked by God to enter the ark.

There were times when God personally spoke to men. Today, one way He speaks to us is through the lives of the men and women of the Bible. He also uses the virtuous lives of others beyond the Bible as great role models for us who are seeking a conscientious relationship with Him.

Women such as Eve, Sarah, Hagar, Rebekah, Ruth, Deborah, Jael, Esther, the Virgin Mary, St. Joan of Arc, and St. Teresa of Kolkata were all powerful women truly used by God. David thanked God for sending Abigail to intercept him from carrying out vengeance. We take notice of the decisions made by these women, how others were impacted, and the lasting legacies left behind.

We learn that Jezebel and her wickedness and pride would never be the best example to follow. Power should never be abused. The more power one possesses, the greater the responsibility one has to demonstrate restraint in all circumstances and show leadership by example. Piety and humility do not necessarily mean weakness. In fact, humility comes before honor.

Some women become very famous, but the majority we never hear about. Every young Jewish girl could not become the mother of Jesus, as Mary did; or St. Teresa, the saint of the gutters, as Agnes did; or queen of England, as Elizabeth II, England's longest-reigning monarch did; or prime minister of Israel, as Golda Meir did in 1969, at age seventy. Every girl cannot become Oprah or Malala, but every girl can be somebody, can reach her full potential.

Looking at the lives of these women, we see the hand of God move in miraculous ways. We recognize some of their decisions and actions did not just affect their world, but have critically spanned the gulf from ancient to contemporary times. Eve's impulsive action to taste of the fruit of the Tree of Knowledge of Good and Evil catapulted mankind into the viciousness of sin. This is an everlasting legacy for all who have been, who are, and who ever will be born of woman—except one: Jesus Christ, our Lord and Savior.

Joan of Arc, young and vulnerable, burned at the stake for wearing masculine attire, was called a sorceress and a heretic. All that she had done for king and country meant nothing to the devious men filled with furor and evil. One solitary goal they shared and sought—her life. The charge of heresy in those days was a weapon utilized by the male-dominated society and church to silence women, by whose leadership they felt threatened.

Only her faith in God enabled Joan to withstand the horrible ordeal of being burned alive. Faith kept Ruth by Naomi's side, refusing to turn back to a life of idolatry after she had tasted and seen that the Lord was good. Only faith in God sustained Agnes Gonxha Bojaxhiu when she felt the strong calling upon her life, left her loved ones, and never looked back. She toiled in the slums of India and became the great advocate of the poor, Mother Teresa, the saint of the gutters.

Today, God is still speaking to us. There are countless women in contemporary times who have exhibited tremendous faith and accomplished great exploits. For years, women have been opting out of just being housewives, either by choice or design. Women have scaled and continue to scale the upper echelons of society, in spite of male dominance.

Malala chose education, breaking the mold of tradition for young Pakistani girls and others worldwide. More and more women are graduating from college and holding their own in the workplace. Even though equal pay has been denied them, several hold very prominent and lucrative positions around the world. Women are holding high-ranking positions in ministry, and a huge number have businesses of their own.

There are the weaker ones like Ann Pettway, whose faith was twisted because of the hard and painful experiences she encountered. In return, she brought tremendous pain to the young parents of Carlina White. Ms. Pettway's lawyers stated she provided well for Carlina, and her crime was not meant to harm, nor was it financially motivated. Her motivation came from her inconsolable desire to birth a child—to have a baby of her own. Though she was sentenced to twelve years in prison, perhaps the court will be lenient and set her free in the near future. This is a prayer for mercy.

There are some women who had faith, enough to propel them to high positions, yet failed those who looked up to them. They allowed their vision to be clouded, their integrity to be compromised, and their appetite for money to dominate and corrupt the sanctity of the offices they pledged to uphold. They lost their way, their honor, and their faith in God, and the support of the status quo. Shimon Peres, former president of Israel, who passed away on September 27, 2016, stated, "The highest degree of wisdom is integrity." When integrity fails, one can no longer be trusted or respected to abide in his or her call to duty. It saddens the heart.

Dilma Rouseff rose to the highest office in Brazil—the

presidency. After serving as chief of staff to the former president, she was elected as the thirty-sixth president in 2010, the first Brazilian woman to achieve that status. As her second term began, scandal arose in the form of bribery charges involving Brazil's national oil company, Petrobras. Cries for her resignation and impeachment filled the international airwaves. She was impeached on August 31, 2016.

From August 2010 until October 2016, Lisa Coico, a brilliant scientist, held the post of the twelfth president of City College of the City University of New York. She had the privilege of being the first alumna of CUNY to serve as president of her alma mater, having graduated in 1976 from Brooklyn College of the City University of New York. Based on a *New York Times* investigative report, she was accused of misusing more than $150,000 of college funds, supposedly spent on furniture and fruit baskets when she took office in 2010.

Students were angry that while they were struggling to make ends meet, the president of their college was siphoning money, in spite of her very liberal salary and benefits package. She unexpectedly resigned on October 7, 2016. In a blog to the Commons Community, Anthony Picciano from *CUNY Education and News Technology* concludes that this is a sad ending to a distinguished career.

Both of these women, with so much to offer to so many, stepped on the wrong side of the law. Hopefully, one day, they can regroup and put their God-given talents to work in some other meaningful way.

We salute contemporaries like Angela Merkel, the first woman to become chancellor of Germany in November 2005, and reelected to second and third terms in 2009 and 2013. She holds a doctorate in physics. She is the daughter of a Lutheran pastor, and religion played a significant role in her upbringing. She became chairwoman of the Christian Democratic Union after the fall of the Berlin Wall in 1989, and was one of the crafters of the European Union.

"While others have turned away, Chancellor Merkel has been stalwart in living the teaching of the gospel by proving she is her brothers' keeper—feeding and sheltering the displaced masses who, without due notice, came within her borders, and providing the support needed by other human beings who may or may not look like her" notes Dr. Monica A. Joseph.

Her commitment to humanitarianism brings to mind none other than St. Teresa, the saint of the gutters. The latter extended her benevolence to the teeming masses of the poor in India. Chancellor Merkel extends hers to the overflow from the crisis in the Middle East between the descendants of Ishmael and Isaac. "And this commandment we have from Him: that he who loves God *must* love his brother also" (1 John 4:21). "But whoever has this world's goods, and sees his brother in need, and shuts up his heart from him, how does the love of God abide in him?" (1 John 3:17). We offer our prayers and wish her the best as she seeks a fourth term in office. May God's will be done in her life.

Janet Yellen, chair of the Federal Reserve of the United States, is another extremely powerful woman of today. A graduate of Brown and Yale Universities, at age seventy, she is the top economist in America, ranked third on the list of *Forbes* Power Women of 2016, first and second being Angela Merkel and Hillary Clinton. "Ms. Yellen is profiled as being unassuming, neither innovator nor wizard. With easy logic and simple speech, she wields her economic strategy as the primary force in the global money market" states Joseph, who also asserts:

"As the responsibility for stabilizing the world's economy fell on her shoulders, Ms. Yellen set about this herculean task without pomp or ceremony. Many have chided her slow and steady steering of the ship of American monetary policy. However, she has never wavered from her advocacy that the economy must work for everybody—poor and not so poor alike." As the chair, her job is to contain inflation and unemployment, issues that substantially affect those in the lower strata of the economy. Many have been able to survive because of the economic decisions she has made.

We salute these elect ladies and thank God for them. They and many other women too numerous to mention prove they know the truth, by demonstrating their love and compassion for their fellowmen. They continue to be great examples to others, especially to the younger ones, like Malala, who are rising up and making themselves heard. "I thank my God through Jesus Christ for you all, that your faith is spoken of throughout the whole world" (Rom. 1:8).

CHAPTER 22

GOD CAN USE ANYONE

E sther, a young maiden, rose to the occasion and saved her people. Joan of Arc was only nineteen when she was burned at the stake, but had led France to several victories over the British. The military strategies she introduced were used by the French to later win the war. Malala was only fifteen when she was shot in the head by the Taliban for advocating for girls' education. God is not looking at age or ethnicity. He is looking for faith, submission, and obedience to His will, whether you are two or ninety-two. He can and will use anyone to bring His plan to fruition. Essentially, it is His will that will be done on earth as in heaven, for of ourselves, we can do nothing.

We see how power, through faith in God, is wielded when we look at the lives of the women I have presented. Then and now, good and bad, their footprints are forever entrenched in the sands of time. They are women who demonstrate not only power, but strength, resilience, and courage. They are women who changed and are changing the course of destiny. They are not just docile creatures. They have been indelibly written into the history books.

From Eve to Malala, we see God at work. Perhaps, most importantly of all, the women whom God elevated and those He continues to elevate over time exhibit humility, obedience, and commitment. If we humble ourselves under the mighty hand of God, He can use us for His glory.

Would you commit your life to God so that He can use you? This is not an insurmountable task. Our mustard seed of faith can be used to accomplish great things. Noah and Rahab saved their entire households through obedience and faith. When the Philippian jailer asked what he should do to be saved, Paul and Silas responded, "Believe on the Lord Jesus Christ, and you will be saved, you and your household" (Acts 16:31).

As air is to our physical well-being, so is faith to our spiritual life. Faith can move mountains. Paul indicates that faith is the underpinning of hope. We can hope for whatever we choose, but the Bible says faith must be accompanied by works. Otherwise our faith is dead, and works cannot be accomplished without faith. As Christians, our very walk with God is based on faith. Faith is our belief that God can deliver when we cry out to Him.

Because of their great faith, Moses, Samuel, Elijah, Elisha, the women portrayed in this book, and many others were successful. Their faith allowed them to persevere and be overcomers. Tamar had the patience to wait for Shelah, the youngest of Judah's sons by Shua, to come to manhood. Her hope was to have a child. When Judah reneged on his promise and did not allow Shelah to marry her, Tamar did not sit and wring her hands. She originated her plan and executed it to perfection. Judah, like all the accusers of the adulteress they brought to Jesus, had to drop his stone and hang his head. Tamar made a powerful statement by exposing Judah and his unfaithfulness.

Oprah, though poor and sexually abused as a child, was able to rise above it all. Growing up in church and constantly hearing the Word of God enabled her to believe enough in herself to finally take control of her life. She states:

> Women have that common bond when it comes to giving up power. I speak to a lot of women now, trying to get them to understand that each of us is responsible for herself. You can read that in books, but it isn't until you come to a spiritual

understanding of who you are—not necessarily a religious feeling, but deep down, the spirit within—that you can begin to take control.[1]

Women and girls, take control of your lives. Put your faith to work. Contend for the faith of the saints of old. Make yourselves available, and God would use you for His ultimate glory. Be a soldier in God's great army. If you should fall, do not stay down for the count. Rise up and keep going, for we stand on the shoulders of many great women who have proven that the weaker vessel, the female, can be used by God to make a difference.

Men and boys, man is the head of woman, as God ordained. This does not mean complete domination of the male over the female. "If Adam could have done it all by himself, he wouldn't have needed Eve ... God made Eve from the rib He took out of Adam ... That means a man will always have something missing without his wife. She completes him."[2] Husbands are commanded by God to love their wives, and in turn, wives must respect their husbands. How beautiful life could be if we followed God's basic instructions.

Women want and need men in their lives, but too often it seems there is a great imbalance. The woman must stifle her independence or personal ambitions in order to accommodate the man. It does not have to be so. God took the rib from Adam's side, thereby establishing that woman is to be at man's side, working in accord with him. The two shall become one.

Mothers and fathers, I reiterate: remember your children look to you for direction as they grow. You cannot afford to fail them. Hattie Mae did not fail Oprah, and, thank God, Vernon and Zelma Winfrey did not. As children come to know the Lord and hear His Word, faith increases and a personal relationship with God develops.

---

[1] Judith Janda Presnall, *Oprah Winfrey* (San Diego, CA: Lucent Books, 1999), 46.

[2] Stormie Omartian, *Praying Through the Deeper Issues of Marriage* (Eugene, OR: Harvest House, 2007), 31.

Kathleen Norris states:

> Faith is still a surprise to me, as I lived without it for so long. Now I believe that it was merely dormant in the years I was not conscious of its presence. And I have become better at trusting that it is there, even when I can't feel it, or when God seems absent from the world ... My new understanding of faith as like energy itself—fluid, always in motion but never constant—has been instructed by the Bible, the Christian theological tradition, and my own experience. Faith is constant, always there, but surging and ebbing, sometimes strongly evident and at other times barely discernible on my spiritual landscape.[3]

Norris mentions she first began to think she might have faith when someone she trusted said he had seen it in her. "In passing he called me 'a woman of faith.' I was stunned; never in my life have I thought of myself that way, and here was a monk saying it to me."[4]

Faith is always there. Everyone, from birth, has a measure of faith—as big as a mustard seed. But faith has to be nurtured. Every experience in life is an opportunity to increase your faith. Faith is the very essence of what you hope will come to pass in your life. Faith must be exercised. It is little Oprah saying that she was going to be somebody someday. It is ten-year-old Malala saying she was not afraid to stand up or to speak out. It is Ruth saying no matter what, she will not turn back. It is Esther saying she will go, and if she perishes, she perishes. It is Hagar returning to a life she abhorred. It is Mary telling the angel to let it be done to her according to God's Word. It is you saying, "I can do all things through Christ who strengthens me" (Phil. 4:13)

---

[3] Kathleen Norris, *Amazing Grace: A Vocabulary of Faith* (New York: Riverhead Books, 1998), 169–70.

[4] Ibid., 173.

God's Word promises that if you wait on the Lord, if you trust in Him, marvelous things would happen. As you build your faith-bridge day by day, wait on the Lord, "that the God of our Lord Jesus Christ, the Father of glory, may give to you the spirit of wisdom and revelation in the knowledge of Him, the eyes of your understanding being enlightened; that you may know what is the hope of His calling" (Eph. 1:17–18). Let your strength be renewed in and by Him. Then you shall surely mount up with eagles' wings and soar to the highest pinnacles, in the name of Jesus!

As ambassadors of Jesus Christ and part of His great army, it is time to rise up and speak. Rise up and be heard! You can no longer be silent. Rise up and be all you can be, for you can do all things through Christ Jesus who strengthens you, even to the saving of your households. "For you were once darkness, but now *you are* light in the Lord. Walk as children of light (for the fruit of the Spirit *is* in all goodness, righteousness, and truth), finding out what is acceptable to the Lord" (Eph. 5:8–10). Pray daily. Do not underestimate the power of prayer!

Paul wrote, "For I am not ashamed of the gospel of Christ, for it is the power of God to salvation for everyone who believes, for the Jew first and also for the Greek. For in it the righteousness of God is revealed from faith to faith; as it is written, "The just shall live by faith" (Rom. 1:16–17). In everything you do, remember: without faith, it is impossible to please God. Aim to please God. He can use anyone.

REFERENCES

Berkhof, Louis. *Introduction to the New Testament.* Grand Rapids, MI: Christian Classics Ethereal Library. http://www.ccel.org/ccel/berkhof/newtestament.html.

Boyce, Rev. James Petigru. *Abstract of Systematic Theology.* Louisville, KY: Chas T. Dearing, 1887. http://founders.org/library/boyce1/toc/.

Calvin, John. *Commentary on Genesis*, vol. 1. Translated and edited by John King. Grand Rapids, MI: Christian Classics Ethereal Library. http://www.ccel.org/ccel/calvin/calcom01.pdf.

Deen, Edith. *All of the Women of the Bible.* San Francisco: HarperCollins, 1955.

Dungan, D. R. *Hermeneutics: A Text-Book.* 2nd edition. Cincinnati, OH: Standard Publishing, 1888.

González-Balado, Jose Luis. *Mother Teresa: In My Own Words.* Liguori, MO: Liguori Publications, 1996.

Gordon, Mary. *Joan of Arc.* New York: Penguin, 2000.

Jamieson, Robert, A. R. Fausset, and David Brown. *Commentary Critical and Explanatory on the Whole Bible.* Grand Rapids, MI: Christian Classic Ethereal Library. http://www.ccel.org/ccel/jamieson/jfb.i.html.

Kelly, Kitty. *Oprah: A Biography.* New York: Crown Publishing Group, a division of Random House, Inc., 2010.

Kuyper, Abraham. *Women of the New Testament: 30 Devotional Messages for Women's Groups*. Grand Rapids, MI: Zondervan, 1934.

Lockyer, Herbert. *All the Women of the Bible*. Grand Rapids, MI: Zondervan, 1988.

Murrell, Stanford E. *A Foundation for Faith: An Introductory Study of Systematic Theology with references to the Baptist Confession of Faith of 1689*. 1998. http://www.ntslibrary.com/PDF%20Books/An%20 Introductory%20Study%20of%20Systematic%20Theology.pdf

Norris, Kathleen. *Amazing Grace: A Vocabulary of Faith*. New York: Riverhead Books, 1998.

Oberman, Kieran. 2015. *War and Poverty*. Politics and International Relations, Faculty Member. United Kingdom: University of Edinburgh. http://www.academia.edu/2328679/War_and_Poverty.

Omartian, Stormie. *Praying Through the Deeper Issues of Marriage*. Eugene, OR: Harvest House, 2007.

Presnall, Judith Janda. *Oprah Winfrey*. San Diego, CA: Lucent Books, 1999.

Richey, Stephen W. *Joan of Arc: A Military Appreciation*. 2000. Albuquerque, NM: Saint

Joan of Arc Center. http://www.stjoan-center.com/military/stephenr.html.

Seeley, Thomas D. *Honeybee Democracy*. Princeton, NJ: Princeton University Press, 2010.

Spoto, Donald. *Joan: The Mysterious Life of the Heretic Who Became a Saint*. San Francisco: HarperCollins, 2007.

Towns, Elmer L. *A Journey Through the Old Testament: The Story of How God Developed His People in the Old Testament*. San Diego, CA: Harcourt Brace, 1989.

Utley, Robert James. *Old Testament Survey 1: Old Testament Written Commentaries*. Bible Lessons International, 2000. http://www. freebiblecommentary.org/old_testament_studies/VOL01AOT/ VOL01AOT_06.html

Vermes, Geza. Introduction to *The Complete Dead Sea Scrolls in English*. Rev. ed. London: Penguin, 2004.

Wesley, John. *Wesley's Notes on the Bible*: *The Old Testament*. Grand Rapids, MI: Christian Classics Ethereal Library.

Whyte, Alexander. *Bible Characters Vol.1–6: The Complete Edition* Dallas, TX: Primedia E-launch, 2011. https://books.google.com/books?id=N9MqM7gDomAC&printsec=frontcover&source=gbs_ge_summary_r&cad=0#v=onepage&q&f=false.

Wood, Joley. Introduction to *Saint Joan*, by Bernard Shaw. London: Penguin, 1924.

Yousafzai, Malala. *I Am Malala*. With Patricia McCormick. New York: Little, Brown, 2014.

APPENDIX I

THE CONFESSION OF FAITH

I f you are not a Christian and wish to accept Jesus Christ as Lord and Savior of your life, it is very simple to do so.

You must believe that you are a sinner and ask God to forgive you your sins, "for all have sinned and come short of the glory of God" (Rom. 3:23).

You must acknowledge that Jesus Christ is the Son of God, that He died on the cross for your sins, was buried, resurrected from the dead, and is sitting at the right hand of the Father in heaven:

> If you confess with your mouth the Lord Jesus and believe in your heart that God has raised Him from the dead, you will be saved. For with the heart one believes unto righteousness, and with the mouth confession is made unto salvation. (Rom. 10:9)

It is as simple as that. Ask Jesus to come into your heart and give you the faith to believe He is your Lord and Savior. He will do it for you. Just believe. Your life will never be the same again.

It is not about religion; it is about your personal relationship with Jesus Christ.

Salvation is free for everyone because Jesus Christ paid our sin debt in full by dying on the cross. We were bought with a price—His death. It takes faith to believe that deliverance from sin comes through Him.

Life is preparation for death. Only you can determine where you will spend eternity, heaven or hell.

APPENDIX II

BAPTISM

When Jesus was eight days old, Joseph and Mary took Him to the temple in Jerusalem to be circumcised and to dedicate Him to the Lord. But when Jesus was thirty years old and about to begin His public ministry, He went to His cousin, John the Baptist, to be baptized in the River Jordan.

> Then Jesus came from Galilee to John at the Jordan to be baptized by him. And John *tried to* prevent Him, saying, "I need to be baptized by You, and are You coming to me?"
>
> But Jesus answered and said to him, "Permit *it to be so* now, for thus it is fitting for us to fulfill all righteousness." Then he allowed Him.
>
> When He had been baptized, Jesus came up immediately from the water; and behold, the heavens were opened to Him, and He saw the Spirit of God descending like a dove and alighting upon Him. And suddenly a voice *came* from heaven, saying, "This is My beloved Son, in whom I am well pleased." (Matt. 3:13–17)

Baptism takes place when you are old enough to consciously make the decision that you want to accept Jesus into your life.

Nicodemus, a Pharisee and a leader of the Jews, came under cover of night to Jesus. Jesus told him he had to be born again in order to see the kingdom of God.

> Nicodemus said to Him, "How can a man be born when he is old? Can he enter a second time into his mother's womb and be born?"

> Jesus answered, "Most assuredly, I say to you, unless one is born of water and the Spirit, he cannot enter the kingdom of God. That which is born of the flesh is flesh, and that which is born of the Spirit is spirit. Do not marvel that I said to you, 'You must be born again.'" (John 3:4–7)

Follow Jesus. He is our Example. He is the Way, the Truth, and the life. You must have that personal relationship with Him.

WHERE WOULD YOU SPEND ETERNITY?
Based on a True Story

The following narrative is true though the name has been changed. John's son-in-law is still alive, living in the United States and can personally testify of this incident.

John was born in Jamaica, West Indies. He grew up, worked hard and made a good life for himself. He owned a big house and drove expensive cars. He lived a life of luxury but God was not a part of it.

John became very ill and family members went to visit him, including his daughter and her husband who lived in New York. John was close to death when they arrived. His son-in-law, a Christian, asked him if he wanted to accept Jesus as his Lord and Savior. He did not reply.

Suddenly, he began to scream over and over, "I don't want to go there! No, No! I don't want to go there!" He was terrified. Those at his bedside were astonished and asked him what he meant. Where did he not want to go? What was he seeing? John did not reply. Again he was asked if he wanted to accept Jesus into his life. It was not too late. He gave no answer and fell asleep.

He awoke screaming the same words, was asked the same

questions, but John remained silent. He fell asleep yet another time and awoke even more agitated, clutching the bed sheets and boisterously proclaiming he did not want to go there. After that third episode, John passed away.

He was silenced forever, leaving his loved ones alarmed and perplexed. Their questions were still unanswered. What did he see that terrified him so? Where did he not want to go? Did he go to that place that literally scared him to death?

God is merciful, kind, full of patience and compassion. He gave John three chances to confess his sins and make it right before he died, but John did not take advantage of the opportunities given him. Before he took his last breath, he refused to accept the mercy God extended to him even to the very end. Hope and mercy are available as long as there is life. But all hope and mercy expire, are completely erased, when we take that final breath on this earth.

Somehow, John lost not only faith, but also hope along the way, and remained obstinate to the very end. He chose to let both time and opportunity slip away from him. But his experience should be a lesson to us all that there is a place to go to after this physical life is ended. Your faith can determine your fate.

The soul never dies. Consequently, we have a choice to make where we will spend eternity, either heaven or hell. We must make that choice while we are alive and able, and be ready to meet our Maker. There are no more opportunities for repentance the moment we take our last breath.

We are all sinners in need of God's grace and forgiveness. He wishes all will have the faith to accept Him and repent of our sins. Therefore,

> "Today, if you will hear His voice,
> Do not harden your hearts." (Heb. 4:7)

> For the word of God *is* living and powerful, and
> sharper than any two-edged sword, piercing even
> to the division of soul and spirit, and of joints
> and marrow, and is a discerner of the thoughts

and intents of the heart. And there is no creature hidden from His sight, but all things *are* naked and open to the eyes of Him to whom we *must give* account. (Heb. 4:12-13)

"Behold, now *is* the accepted time; behold, now *is* the day of salvation (2 Cor. 6:7). Therefore, my beloved ... work out your own salvation with fear and trembling" (Phil. 2:12). There should be no delay for tomorrow is not promised. Please, do not harden your heart like John did. Let today be your day of salvation. It is free for every last one of us! It is the greatest gift given to us through Jesus, the Messiah—eternal life.

Where do you plan to spend eternity?

ABOUT THE AUTHOR

D r. Jacqueline George, an educator for over thirty years, holds a doctorate of philosophy in biblical studies from Newburgh Theological Seminary, a master's degree in administration from Touro College, and a master's degree in voice performance from New York University. Ordained as a minister of God in 2010, she remains active in ministry. Her pastimes are reading the Bible and writing.

INDEX

Printed in the United States
By Bookmasters